The 365-Day
Bible
Word
Game
Challenge

The 365 Day
Bible
Word
Game
Challenge

A
Bible Puzzle
for every day
of the year!

BARBOUR
PUBLISHING

Published by Barbour Publishing, Inc., P.O. Box 719, Uhrichsville, Ohio 44683 www.barbourbooks.com

Our mission is to publish and distribute inspirational products offering exceptional value and biblical encouragement to the masses.

ECPA Member of the
Evangelical Christian
Publishers Association

Introduction

Welcome to *The 365-Day Bible Word Game Challenge*! Here you'll find an enjoyable word game for every day of the year, each one based on the greatest book of all time—the Bible.

Featuring eight types of puzzles, *The 365-Day Bible Word Game Challenge* promises hours of educational fun. Here's how to play each game:

Drop Two Puzzles (see Day 1): Remove two letters from each seven-letter word in the left-hand column to create a new five-letter word (you may need to rearrange the remaining letters). Put the two dropped letters into the spaces to the right of the blanks. Then use these letters to spell out a phrase or sentence from the Bible. Puzzles designed by Dorothy Pryse.

Decoders (see Day 2): Using the decoder grid, uncover a Bible verse for each puzzle. For each two-digit number in the puzzle, find a corresponding letter by matching the first number with the vertical column and the second number with the horizontal row. Place all letters in the puzzle blanks, and the verse will appear. Puzzles designed by Christy Barritt.

Acrostics (see Day 3): Read the definition in the left-hand column and write the word it describes in the right-hand column. Then place the coded letters from the right-hand column in the puzzle form following to spell out the verse indicated. Puzzles designed by Christy Barritt.

Scrambled Circles (see Day 4): Unscramble the words from the list provided, placing the corrected words in the blanks corresponding with the numbers. Then use the circled letters to answer the question following. Puzzles designed by Ken Save.

CryptoScriptures (see Day 5): Each of the CryptoScriptures is a Bible verse in substitution code. For example, JEHOVAH might become M P X S T Q X if M is substituted for J, P for E, X for H, and so on. One way to break the code is to look for repeated letters: E, T, A, O, N, R, and I are the most often used. A single letter is usually A or I. OF, IT, and IS are common two-letter words. Try THE or AND for a three-letter group. The code is different for each CryptoScripture. Puzzles designed by Sharon Y. Brown.

Spotty Headlines (see Day 6): Fill in the missing letters of each "headline," which relates to a Bible story. Then unscramble the letters you've added to the headline to form a name, which is the subject of the headline. Puzzles designed by Sara Stoker.

Bible Quotations (see Day 7): Place the letters in each column into the puzzle grid preceding to form words. The letters may or may not fit into the grid in the same order in which they're given; black spaces indicate the ends of words. When a letter has been used, cross it off and do not use it again. When the grid has been properly filled in, you'll be able to read a Bible verse by scanning the lines of the grid from left to right. Puzzles designed by G. Rebecca Shodin.

Telephone Scrambles (see Day 8): Each set of telephone push-buttons contains a hidden Bible word—and you'll need to determine which letter of each three-letter combination is part of the word. Puzzles designed by Nancy Bernhard.

Anagrams (see Day 180): Unscramble the letters of the word or phrase given to create another word or phrase from the Bible. Puzzles designed by Paul Kent.

Now you're all set for a year's worth of Bible puzzle fun. Enjoy!

Acts

Word	Clue	Answer	#		
~~BLEMISH~~	Facial move	Smile	1.	B	H
~~DECEASE~~	Packaged	Cased	2.	K	E
~~CHATHAM~~	Igniter	Match	3.	A	H
~~OVERACT~~	Sketch	Trace	4.	O	V
~~GENERAL~~	Stove	Range	5.	E	L
~~NIBBLED~~	Holy book	Bible	6.	B	D
~~SEABIRD~~	Facial hair	Beard	7.	S	I
~~PLUMOSE~~	Feather	Plume	8.	O	S
~~PIERCED~~	Wept	cried	9.	P	E
~~ENDWISE~~	Breezes	Winds	10.	E	E
NESTING	Burn lightly	Sting	11.	N	E
~~UNHOPED~~	16 ounces	Pound	12.	H	e
~~UNYOKED~~	Northern Territory	Yukon	13.	E	D

H E B l e s s e d D A V i X

D _ _ _ _ _ _ _ _ _ _ _ _

1 2 3 4 5 6 7 8 9 10 11 12 13

Psalm 27:14

	1	2	3	4	5
1	A	K	E	L	T
2	N	H	F	J	U
3	I	Y	B	X	G
4	O	S	M	D	W
5	R	C	Q	V	P

45-11-31-15   41-21   15-22-13   14-41-51-44:   33-13

41-23   35-41-41-44   52-41-25-51-11-35-13,

11-21-44   22-13   42-22-11-14-14

42-15-51-13-21-35-15-22-13-21   15-22-31-21-13

22-13-11-51-15:   45-11-31-15,   31   42-11-32,   41-21

15-22-13   14-41-51-44.

Day 2

ROMANS 14:19

A sign, symbol, or indication

M a r k
30 10 11 36

Fabric that represents one's country

F l a g
7 26 1 20

Exhibiting much weight

H e a v y
16 32 6 23 39

An auxiliary form of the verb will

w o u l d
8 24 2 18 13

To type out something in full

M a n u s c r i p t
33 3 29 17 9 4 25 21 12 28

transcribe

Stubborn continuance

S t r o n g w i l l d
22 35 14 38 27 19 37 5 15 31 34

Persistance

26-32-33   2-38   33-16-28-25-5-7-24-11-5

7-24-26-18-24-8   1-7-33-28-11   33-16-32

37-16-21-17-20-19   8-16-21-4-16   30-29-36-28

7-24-25   22-35-29-31-35,   1-17-13

33-16-21-17-20-9   8-16-34-3-28-8-27-37-16

24-15-28   30-1-39   28-13-27-7-39

6-17-24-33-16-28-25.

Scrambled Circles

1. SJUSE
2. ERPOTHPS
3. DHWSASO
4. SLDNAA
5. ZATPBEI
6. APALHNIT
7. REAABPL
8. PIRSTI
9. RESHSEIAP
10. UEDETBSATI
11. LSTA

He really lost his head over Jesus. Who was he?

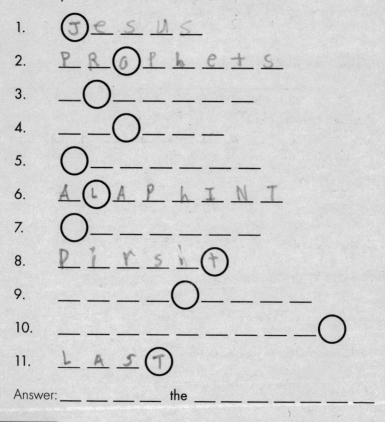

1. (J) e s u s
2. P R (O) p h e t s
3. _ (○) _ _ _ _
4. _ _ (○) _ _ _
5. (○) _ _ _ _ _
6. A (L) A P h I N I
7. (○) _ _ _ _ _
8. P i r s h (t)
9. _ _ _ (○) _ _ _ _
10. _ _ _ _ _ _ _ _ (○)
11. L A S (T)

Answer: ___ __ __ __ the __ __ __ __ __ __ __ __

1. QVY OUGJ GJ OUK RKJJNAK
   OUNO ZK UKNYS QYVR OUK
   IKAGBBGBA, OUNO HK JUVPWS
   WVLK VBK NBVOUKY.

2. WV ZBZCN FMWVY YWBZ
   FMEVHO: RDC FMWO WO FMZ
   LWXX DR YDP WV KMCWOF
   QZOSO KDVKZCVWVY NDG.

3. ILER RWNIL ILJ SZYQ ILJ VNMU
   ZC NRYWJS, WMQ LNR YJQJJGJY
   ILJ SZYQ ZC LZRIR; N WG
   ILJ CNYRI, WMQ N WG ILJ SWRI;
   WMQ HJRNQJ GJ ILJYJ NR MZ
   UZQ.

[handwritten notes, partially legible:]
1 It S _ M _ M S _ E _ E M M _ Q E
S _ S _ E _ E _ _ Q E _ _ _ S _ E
_ E Q _ _ _ _ _ Q S _ S X _ M _ T P _ Q
_ t _ _ t h E _ _ t S _ E _

Old Testament Headlines

1.

BLI⬤D C⬤PTIVE
DE⬤TR⬤Y⬤ TE⬤PLE

<u>N</u> <u>A</u> <u>S</u> <u>o</u> <u>D</u> <u>m</u> X

2.

LUN⬤TIC ⬤AS
TH⬤USANDS OF A⬤IMALS

<u>A</u> <u>h</u> <u>o</u> <u>n</u> ✓
Noha

3.

K⬤NG ⬤OUBLY
⬤IOLATES SACRE⬤ L⬤WS

<u>I</u> <u>D</u> <u>V</u> <u>D</u> <u>A</u> ✓
DAvid

John 1:4

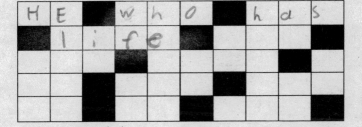

H	E		w	h	o		h	a	s
	l	i	f	e					

A ~~L~~ ~~L~~ T F I ~~A~~ ~~A~~ N ~~S~~
~~H~~ S ~~E~~ O E M ~~F~~ ~~W~~ A W
I T H L E M N D G
T N F ~~H~~ E I
~~H~~ I L

He who has life

ALLEGORIES

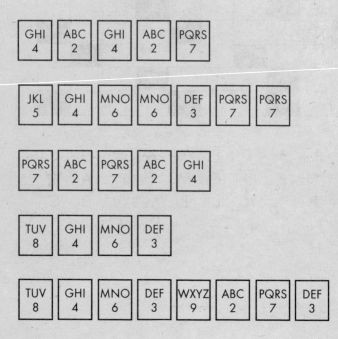

Scrambled Circles

1. REVIDSE ~~Revised~~ X Diverse
2. EIMT Time ✓
3. MAELF ~~Female~~ X Flame
4. TNNIECA
5. REMNATG
6. DUCKELP Plucked ✓
7. DENIEGECX
8. LESEHW wheels ✓

"God is with us." Another name for the coming Messiah.

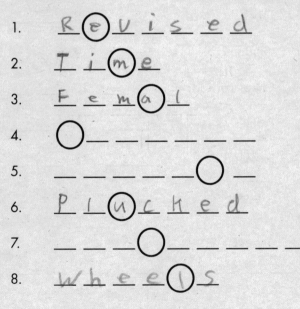

1. R E(e)V I S E D
2. T I M(m)E
3. F E M A(a)L
4. (O)_ _ _ _ _ _
5. _ _ _ _ (O)_ _
6. P L(u)U C K E D
7. _ _ (O)_ _ _ _
8. W H E E L(l)S

Answer: E M A _ _ U _ L

Day
9

Drop Two

LIONESS   Phone wires   _____   1. __ __

SULPHUR   Soft   _____   2. __ __

LECTERN   Choose   _____   3. __ __

EREMITE   Joint   _____   4. __ __

FEMORAL   Enclose photo   _____   5. __ __

SUAVELY   Ointment   _____   6. __ __

SHARPER   Grammar   _____   7. __ __

GRANITE   Teach   _____   8. __ __

LEATHER   Gladden   _____   9. __ __

AMERICA   Cheese or soda   _____   10. __ __

TREACLE   Profit   _____   11. __ __

SHERIFF   Fast-food   _____   12: __ __

BURGESS   Crescendo   _____   13. __ __

__ __ __ __ __ __ __ __ __ __ __ __ __

__ __ __ __ __ __ __ __ __ __ __ __ __

1   2   3   4   5   6   7   8   9   10   11   12   13

Day 10

1 Corinthians 3:16

	1	2	3	4	5
1	A	K	E	L	T
2	N	H	F	J	U
3	I	Y	B	X	G
4	O	S	M	D	W
5	R	C	Q	V	P

12-21-41-45   32-13   21-41-15   15-22-11-15

32-13   11-51-13   15-22-13   15-13-43-55-14-13

41-23   35-41-44,   11-21-44   15-22-11-15   15-22-13

42-55-31-51-31-15   41-23   35-41-44

44-45-13-14-14-13-15-22   31-21   32-41-25?

Acrostic

1 Corinthians 15:58

A metal object worn over the finger while sewing

____ ____ ____ ____ ____ ____ ____
10 33 18 5 1 28 24

Time spent on the job

____ ____ ____ ____ ____ ____ ____
29 34 9 25 4 21 17

A feeling that leads to scratching

____ ____ ____ ____ ____
38 42 2 13 44

To work more hours than you've been scheduled

____ ____ ____ ____ ____ ____ ____ ____
11 41 20 32 15 27 6 12

Moved from one location to another

____ ____ ____ ____ ____ ____ ____ ____ ____ ____ ____
36 39 3 22 14 19 31 8 37 45 23

Lacking worth

____ ____ ____ ____ ____ ____ ____
26 43 35 7 30 16 40

15-13-20-8-24-19-11-32-12,   6-44

1-35-7-11-41-31-23   1-9-30-10-33-32-35-22,

1-45   44-20   16-36-30-23-19-3-43-15,

26-21-6-34-41-24-3-1-28-45,   3-28-29-3-44-14

3-1-11-26-22-23-27-22-17   38-22

42-13-20   29-34-37-25   11-19   42-13-24

28-34-39-23.

1. ERSPEVREE
2. SNAAPG
3. HRRETOB
4. IERLVETANO
5. NSIS
6. LSUNEFLS
7. LSPIEWFHLO

This church had a golden lampstand named after it.

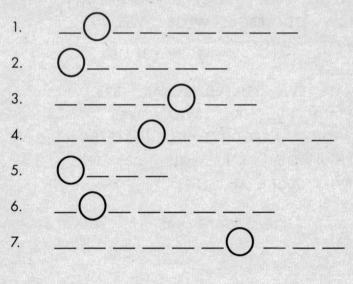

1. __ ⬤ __ __ __ __ __ __

2. ⬤ __ __ __ __ __

3. __ __ __ __ ⬤ __ __

4. __ __ __ ⬤ __ __ __ __ __ __

5. ⬤ __ __ __

6. __ ⬤ __ __ __ __ __ __

7. __ __ __ __ __ __ ⬤ __ __ __

Answer: __ __ __ __ __ __ __

1. QTDN   NCKQT   QTY   VZSI,   VYQ
   GZQ   QTY   UKNY   ACG   EVZSW   KG
   TKN   UKNIZA,   GYKQTYS   VYQ   QTY
   AKETQW   ACG   EVZSW   KG   TKN
   AKETQ,   VYQ   GZQ   QTY   SKMT   ACG
   EVZSW   KG   TKN   SKMTYN.

2. PLO   WFGI   WFPW   ELDV   WFI   LPSG
   VZMM   RJW   WFGZC   WCJYW   ZL
   WFGG: TDC   WFDJ,   MDCO,   FPYW
   LDW   TDCYPEGL   WFGS   WFPW
   YGGE   WFGG.

3. XAT   BVJ   YTJKEVDZQ   AX   BVJ
   ETAHH   DH   BA   BVJO   BVKB
   YJTDHV   XAAGDHVZJHH;   UPB   PZBA
   PH   RVDEV   KTJ   HKIJS   DB   DH
   BVJ   YARJT   AX   QAS.

Day
14

Old Testament Headlines

1.

**●ELIEVING W●NDERER P●O●ISED
L●ND FOR ●IS M●NY HEIRS**

— — — — — — —

2.

**FIR●T KING OF ISRO●●
COMMITS S●ICIDE**

— — — —

3.

**C●PTIVE BOY'S THR●E FRIEN●S
DE●IVERED FROM F●RE U●HURT**

— — — — — —

Isaiah 12:5

```
T   H   O   E   U   X   C   A
G   S   L   T   E   O   H   T   O   H
R   I   O   N   E   L   H   E   D   O   T   E
A   R   N   N   L   W   H   N   E   A   T   N
L   D   E   H   W   H   I   E   A   N   I   S
S   K   H   H   H   T   I   N   R   I   H   F
O   L   N   G   T       R   T   H   I   E
    L   N       T           R       E
    T
```

PRISONERS

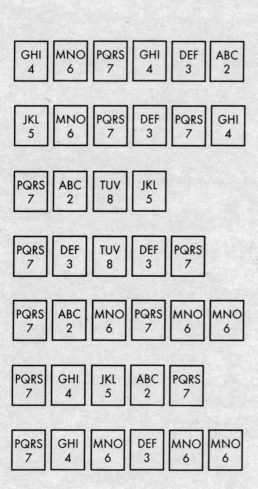

| GHI 4 | MNO 6 | PQRS 7 | GHI 4 | DEF 3 | ABC 2 |

| JKL 5 | MNO 6 | PQRS 7 | DEF 3 | PQRS 7 | GHI 4 |

| PQRS 7 | ABC 2 | TUV 8 | JKL 5 |

| PQRS 7 | DEF 3 | TUV 8 | DEF 3 | PQRS 7 |

| PQRS 7 | ABC 2 | MNO 6 | PQRS 7 | MNO 6 | MNO 6 |

| PQRS 7 | GHI 4 | JKL 5 | ABC 2 | PQRS 7 |

| PQRS 7 | GHI 4 | MNO 6 | DEF 3 | MNO 6 | MNO 6 |

Day 17

Scrambled Circles

1. SMREAT
2. TBASES
3. ESNVE
4. NOKMDIG
5. TOSOR
6. COAOSNIC
7. EPKSA
8. IRNGE

What plant with purple or white flowers is used for medicines?

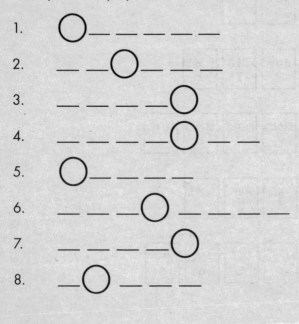

Answer: __ __ __ __ __ __ __ __ __

ZECHARIAH

ISHMAEL	Eating times	_____	1. ___ ___
OVERSAW	Relish	_____	2. ___ ___
ALIFORM	Plants	_____	3. ___ ___
BOILING	Game	_____	4. ___ ___
PEDICLE	Music score	_____	5. ___ ___
MADNESS	Titles	_____	6. ___ ___
FITCHEW	Leader	_____	7. ___ ___
POACHER	To dry	_____	8. ___ ___
HERSELF	Transparent	_____	9. ___ ___
SHALLOT	Sandbar	_____	10. ___ ___
ETHICAL	Shoe grip	_____	11. ___ ___
REAGENT	Large	_____	12. ___ ___
DEEPEST	Hasten	_____	13. ___ ___

___ ___ ___ ___ ___ ___ ___ ___ ___ ___ ___ ___ ___

___ ___ ___ ___ ___ ___ ___ ___ ___ ___ ___ ___ ___

1   2   3   4   5   6   7   8   9   10   11   12   13

Day 19

1 Corinthians 13:11

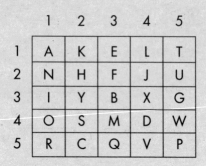

33-25-15   45-22-13-21   31   33-13-52-11-43-13   11

43-11-21,   31   55-25-15   11-45-11-32

52-22-31-14-44-31-42-22   15-22-31-21-35-42.

MATTHEW 6:24

To put something over something else

$\overline{}$ $\overline{}$ $\overline{}$ $\overline{}$ $\overline{}$
21   11   34   5   27

The place where one lives

$\overline{}$ $\overline{}$ $\overline{}$ $\overline{}$
33   12   4   28

Making no noise

$\overline{}$ $\overline{}$ $\overline{}$ $\overline{}$ $\overline{}$ $\overline{}$
6   32   17   30   22   15

Microscopic plants and animals that fish feed off of

$\overline{}$ $\overline{}$ $\overline{}$ $\overline{}$ $\overline{}$ $\overline{}$ $\overline{}$ $\overline{}$
23   7   20   1   29   16   26   10

Having lots of money

$\overline{}$ $\overline{}$ $\overline{}$ $\overline{}$ $\overline{}$ $\overline{}$ $\overline{}$
13   35   8   31   3   24   19

Melted cheese used as a dip

$\overline{}$ $\overline{}$ $\overline{}$ $\overline{}$ $\overline{}$ $\overline{}$
2   25   14   18   9   36

1-12   4-20-10   21-20-10   6-35-27-34-28   15-13-26

4-8-6-16-30-27-6:   2-25-27   35-32-3-24-5-27   24-35

13-32-17-31   33-20-15-28   15-24-35   12-1-36,

8-22-18   17-11-34-28   16-24-28   25-3-24-5-27;

12-27   28-17-6-30   24-35   13-32-7-31   33-26-31-18

3-11   16-24-35   12-1-28,   8-14-18   18-30-6-23-32-6-30

16-24-28   26-16-24-35-27.

1. OPLEEP
2. IOGNRANG
3. NDSRCOEI
4. ROVGSEIEN
5. YRECM
6. FLINSU
7. GTESLURG
8. NTOLCOR
9. IPNSAOSS

She may have had the same name, but she was *not* the wife of the famous singer. Who was she?

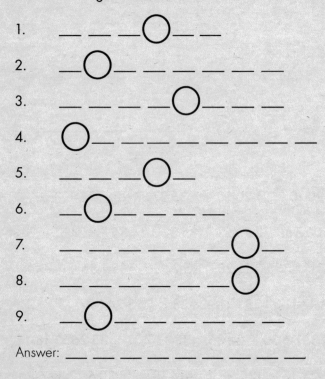

1. __ __ __ Ο __ __

2. __ Ο __ __ __ __ __ __ __

3. __ __ __ __ Ο __ __ __

4. Ο __ __ __ __ __ __ __ __ __

5. __ __ __ Ο __

6. __ Ο __ __ __ __

7. __ __ __ __ __ Ο __

8. __ __ __ __ __ __ Ο

9. __ Ο __ __ __ __ __

Answer: __ __ __ __ __ __ __ __ __

1. OYXR   WXOXH   VRJ   OYX   IOYXH
   VWIBOUXB   VRBCXHXJ   VRJ   BVSJ,
   CX   IGFYO   OI   IAXM   FIJ   HVOYXH
   OYVR   LXR.

2. KRUO   WOOY   KWRK   QO   YS   ZSK
   QSPX   RIDG   MOJSXO   DOZ,   KS   MO
   GOOZ   SJ   KWOD: SKWOXLTGO   QO
   WRFO   ZS   XOLRXY   SJ   QSPX   JRKWOX
   LWTAW   TG   TZ   WORFOZ.

3. FYT   CBD   ZEGT,   BD   WC   WN   CBFC
   TECB   KE   ODVEGD   CBDD: BD   QWZZ
   OD   QWCB   CBDD,   BD   QWZZ   YEC
   VFWZ   CBDD,   YDWCBDG   VEGNFID   CBDD:
   VDFG   YEC,   YDWCBDG   OD   TWNSFADT.

OLD TESTAMENT HEADLINES

1.

**FIRST ●AN CON●EMNS
●LL FUTURE GENER●TIONS**

— — — —

2.

**●LAVE BABY RAIS●D AS
PHARA●H'S ●IGHTY ●ON**

— — — — —

3.

**●UST PROP●ET
L●MENTS D●STRUCT●ON OF
TH● LO●D'S TE●PLE**

— — — — — — — —

**Day
24**

3 John 1:4

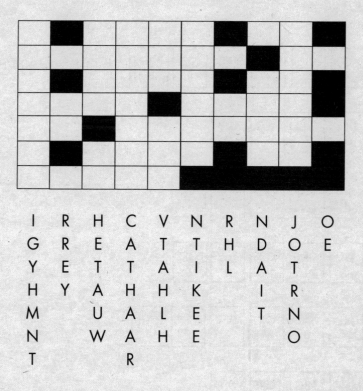

I R H C V N R N J O
G R E A T T H D O E
Y E T T A I L A T R
H Y A H H K L I T N
M U H L E E T R O
N W A E E N O
T A R

Telephone Scrambles

GENEALOGIES

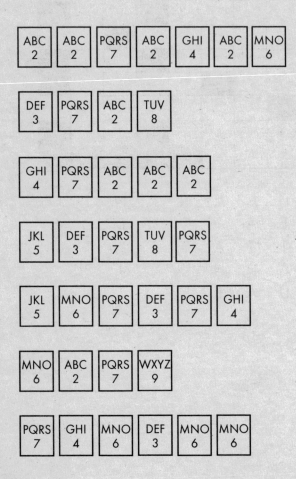

Day 26

Scrambled Circles

1. SGAEILRLE
2. SOSTP
3. NAELEV
4. NEBEETW
5. ROTSIES
6. DRENDUH
7. EHERT

8. RARONW
9. TORHN
10. RADOB
11. TUCIB
12. DAEH
13. RAMBEHC
14. SAERHC

A new commandment to live by.

1. __ __ __ ⃝ __ __ __ __ __
2. __ ⃝ __ __ __
3. __ __ __ ⃝ __ __ __
4. __ ⃝ __ __ __ __ __
5. __ __ ⃝ __ __ __
6. __ __ ⃝ __ __ __ __
7. __ __ __ ⃝ __
8. __ ⃝ __ __ __ __
9. ⃝ __ __ __ __ __
10. __ __ ⃝ __ __ __
11. __ __ __ ⃝ __
12. ⃝ __ __ __ __
13. __ __ __ __ __ ⃝ __
14. __ ⃝ __ __ __ __

Answer: __ __ __ __ __   __ __ __ __

__ __ __ __ __ __ __

Drop Two

Colossians

ADAPTER	Bandaged	_____	1. ___ ___
NASTIER	Step	_____	2. ___ ___
DISTAFF	Unyielding	_____	3. ___ ___
LEGHORN	Hopeless person	_____	4. ___ ___
MENTHOL	1/12 year	_____	5. ___ ___
PLICATE	Put	_____	6. ___ ___
SCATHED	Performed	_____	7. ___ ___
BRAIDED	Anxiety	_____	8. ___ ___
ENABLED	Knife part	_____	9. ___ ___
FLAGGED	Woods opening	_____	10. ___ ___
STETSON	Encampment	_____	11. ___ ___

___ ___ ___ ___ ___ ___ ___ ___ ___ ___ ___

___ ___ ___ ___ ___ ___ ___ ___ ___ ___ ___

1   2   3   4   5   6   7   8   9   10   11

Day 28

Ecclesiastes 12:13

	1	2	3	4	5
1	A	K	E	L	T
2	N	H	F	J	U
3	I	Y	B	X	G
4	O	S	M	D	W
5	R	C	Q	V	P

14-13-15   25-42   22-13-11-51   15-22-13

52-41-21-52-14-25-42-31-41-21   41-23   15-22-13

45-22-41-14-13   43-11-15-15-13-51:   23-13-11-51

35-41-44,   11-21-44   12-13-13-55   22-31-42

52-41-43-43-11-21-44-43-13-21-15-42:   23-41-51

15-22-31-42   31-42   15-22-13   45-22-41-14-13

44-25-15-32   41-23   43-11-21.

Acrostic

ISAIAH 1:18

A personal wardrobe

$\overline{34}$ $\overline{7}$ $\overline{21}$ $\overline{16}$ $\overline{1}$ $\overline{30}$ $\overline{12}$

The location of something

$\overline{26}$ $\overline{5}$ $\overline{31}$ $\overline{17}$ $\overline{13}$ $\overline{35}$ $\overline{4}$ $\overline{42}$ $\overline{25}$ $\overline{9}$ $\overline{20}$

A place suitable to the person in it

$\overline{38}$ $\overline{6}$ $\overline{43}$ $\overline{32}$ $\overline{44}$

A wide variety of food

$\overline{33}$ $\overline{8}$ $\overline{36}$ $\overline{14}$ $\overline{27}$ $\overline{18}$ $\overline{3}$ $\overline{41}$ $\overline{11}$ $\overline{29}$ $\overline{23}$

Full of spices

$\overline{10}$ $\overline{40}$ $\overline{2}$ $\overline{22}$ $\overline{19}$

A fictitious tale

$\overline{37}$ $\overline{24}$ $\overline{39}$ $\overline{15}$ $\overline{28}$

34-21-8-30   38-21-26,   35-38-23   7-31-9   25-37

14-44-18-37-11-38   16-21-27-44-16-32-13-15,   12-18-2-24-5

16-32-44   7-36-15-23:   16-32-21-25-27-5   19-11-25-17

20-2-38-37   41-30   35-20   10-22-18-17-7-30-9,

24-5-30-28   12-5-35-7-7   4-31   35-10   26-1-6-16-13

35-20   33-38-42-26.

1. ZAEBITP
2. NWEDOR
3. RCYESRO
4. TYHUO
5. RDCEEAL

6. RNESKTIC
7. LUYMPTIL
8. RAHTE
9. DHNSA

This prophet was the son of Berechiah.

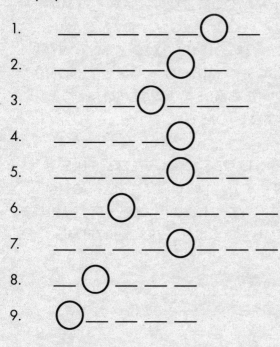

1. __ __ __ __ __ ◯ __

2. __ __ __ __ ◯ __

3. __ __ __ ◯ __ __ __

4. __ __ __ __ ◯

5. __ __ __ __ ◯ __ __

6. __ __ ◯ __ __ __ __

7. __ __ __ __ ◯ __ __

8. __ ◯ __ __ __

9. ◯ __ __ __ __

Answer: __ __ __ __ __ __ __ __ __

1. V PVW VZFU UT OUPVW LEVL
   EVLE V KVPSZSVT FMSTSL, UT LEVL
   SF V OSIVTX, FEVZZ FBTDZQ GD
   MBL LU XDVLE: LEDQ FEVZZ FLUWD
   LEDP OSLE FLUWDF: LEDST GZUUX
   FEVZZ GD BMUW LEDP.

2. YZR FA MDYOO TXPQ AX VYMM,
   ADYA LSXP XZQ ZQG PXXZ AX
   YZXADQS, YZR LSXP XZQ MYWWYAD
   AX YZXADQS, MDYOO YOO LOQMD
   TXPQ AX GXSMDFV WQLXSQ PQ,
   MYFAD ADQ OXSR.

3. ULQT OE EZQT RXZK EZR, LKS
   FTLYK ZN OT; NZY V LO OTTQ
   LKS FZHFE VK ITLYU: LKS ET MILFF
   NVKS YTMU RKUZ EZRY MZRFM.

OLD TESTAMENT HEADLINES

1.

**F●RST MURDER
●OMMITTED O● E●RTH
BY A MAN**

— — — —

2.

**Y●UNG BROT●ER ●ULLED
FROM PIT AND UN●USTLY
●OLD AS SLAV●**

— — — — — —

3.

**KING THREATE●ING T● CUT
CHI●D IN TW● ●AY SETTLE
●WNERSHIP DI●PUTE**

— — — — — — —

REVELATION 22:12


```
Q   D   A   Y   O   L   L   L   A   O
D   U   I   S   H   R   S   M   A   E
M   A   M   T   H   W   D   E   H   N
R   A   I   E   O   R   B   I   V   G
E   K   V   C   R   Y   O   M   A   N
L   E   C   N   D   C   Y   I   N   R
D   D   S   I   K   A   I   W   W   O
        C       I   E   T   H   B
        S           G       E
```

MEASUREMENTS

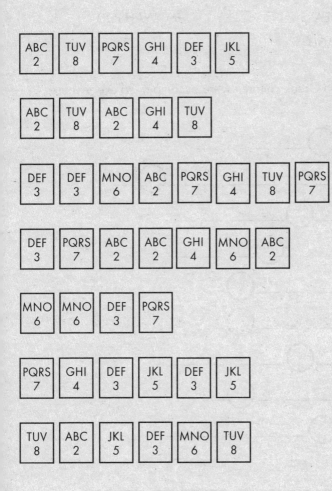

Scrambled Circles

1. NORAG
2. NESTUCHT
3. TENLAM
4. DREAPS
5. NADH
6. LINAS
7. NADERG
8. NODUB
9. WAHSOD

Well-to-do Greek children were accompanied everywhere by these.

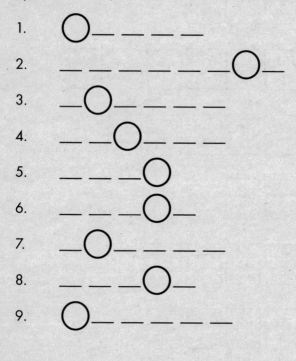

1. ⭕ __ __ __ __

2. __ __ __ __ __ __ ⭕ __

3. __ ⭕ __ __ __ __

4. __ __ ⭕ __ __ __

5. __ __ __ ⭕

6. __ __ __ ⭕ __

7. __ ⭕ __ __ __ __

8. __ __ __ ⭕ __

9. ⭕ __ __ __ __ __

Answer: __ __ __ __ __ __ __ __ __

1 PETER

STEALTH	Warms	_____	1. ___ ___
HAPLOID	Checked	_____	2. ___ ___
ERODENT	Softened sound	_____	3. ___ ___
WRAPPED	Document	_____	4. ___ ___
OPERATE	Candle	_____	5. ___ ___
RAMPANT	Florida city	_____	6. ___ ___
DRAFTED	Not before	_____	7. ___ ___
OEDIPUS	Caught site of	_____	8. ___ ___
FRESHET	Bed cover	_____	9. ___ ___
TRAIPSE	Mates	_____	10. ___ ___
NIGHTLY	Fibbing	_____	11. ___ ___
STROPHE	Harbour towns	_____	12. ___ ___

___ ___ ___ ___ ___ ___ ___ ___ ___ ___ ___ ___

___ ___ ___ ___ ___ ___ ___ ___ ___ ___ ___ ___

1 2 3 4 5 6 7 8 9 10 11 12

1 Thessalonians 5:9

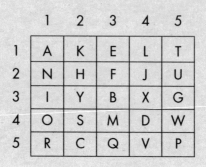

	1	2	3	4	5
1	A	K	E	L	T
2	N	H	F	J	U
3	I	Y	B	X	G
4	O	S	M	D	W
5	R	C	Q	V	P

23-41-51   35-41-44   22-11-15-22   21-41-15

11-55-55-41-31-21-15-13-44   25-42   15-41

45-51-11-15-22,   33-25-15   15-41   41-33-15-11-31-21

42-11-14-54-11-15-31-41-21   33-32   41-25-51

14-41-51-44   24-13-42-25-42   52-22-51-31-42-15.

Psalm 1:3

Charmed by an irresistable appeal

—32— —5— —40— —27— —16— —20— —1— —38— —10— —42—

The projects a child does outside school

—36— —4— —17— —30— —41— —24— —39— —23—

Misty

—43— —18— —22— —6— —33—

Clear, transparent quartz

—7— —11— —29— —31— —15— —21— —3—

Looking on the bright side

—44— —12— —37— —2— —14— —28— —8— —34— —19— —25—

A baby rabbit

—45— —26— —13— —9— —35—

5-13-42   36-30   31-36-5-3-3   45-30

3-16-23-10   21   27-11-10-30

40-3-5-9-37-10-42   45-33   34-36-30

39-28-20-10-39-8   44-43   41-21-27-30-11,

27-36-5-27   45-39-16-13-22-10-34-36

43-4-39-38-36   36-2-8   43-11-26-19-15   16-13

36-28-31   8-30-1-31-18-9.

1. EPLEOP   6. TOSUATC

2. ETARG   7. ODBLEH

3. EISNAREC   8. SAPS

4. ERERTOS   9. TMSEI

5. REUDVO

Such a wind was worth the wait.

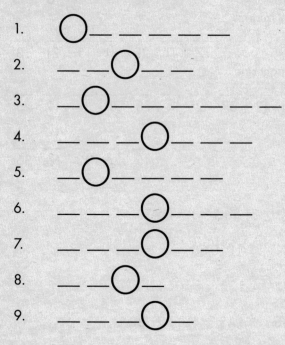

1. ◯ __ __ __ __ __

2. __ __ ◯ __ __

3. __ ◯ __ __ __ __ __ __

4. __ __ __ ◯ __ __ __

5. __ ◯ __ __ __ __

6. __ __ __ ◯ __ __ __

7. __ __ __ ◯ __ __

8. __ __ ◯ __

9. __ __ __ ◯ __

Answer: __ __ __ __ __ __ __ __ __ __

1. XNB DWM IWFFUPMUBZ ZKJ VWHU BWQOTM NJ, KP BZOB, QZKVU QU QUTU LUB JKPPUTJ, IZTKJB MKUM YWT NJ.

2. UEE CQZGDKSZH GC AGLHY JN GYCDGZUKGRY RP ARV, UYV GC DZRPGKUJEH PRZ VRQKZGYH, PRZ ZHDZRRP, PRZ QRZZHQKGRY, PRZ GYCKZSQKGRY GY ZGATKHRSCYHCC.

3. R ZSIQ MJXM, QJXMVITATC BIW WITMJ, RM VJXFF PT NIC TATC: SIMJRSB DXS PT OEM MI RM, SIC XSK MJRSB MXZTS NCIL RM: XSW BIW WITMJ RM, MJXM LTS VJIEFW NTXC PTNICT JRL.

Old Testament Headlines

1.

**PROP●ET HAS BE●UN
ENCOUR●G●N● EX-C●PTIVES TO
REBUILD TEMPLE**

— — — — — — —

2.

**P●●EST RENEWS
●EAL TOW●RD T●MPLE
RE●AB AMONGST T●E
EX-●●PTIVES**

— — — — — — — —

3.

**OLD CHILDLESS M●N
●ELIEVES PR●●ISE TO
●●VE M●NY CHILD●EN**

— — — — — —

Day
42

ECCLESIASTES 3:1

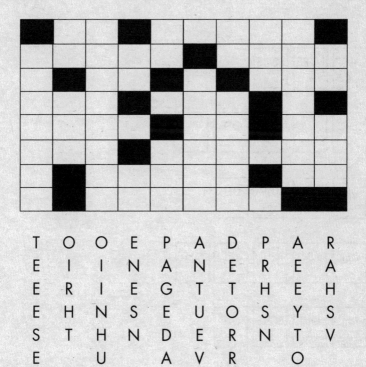

```
T   O   O   E   P   A   D   P   A   R
E   I   I   N   A   T   E   R   E   A
E   R   I   E   G   T   T   H   E   H
E   H   N   S   E   U   O   S   Y   S
S   T   H   N   D   E   R   N   T   V
E       U       A   V   R       O
T       Y           V   E       E
        M
```

Telephone Scrambles

ANIMALS IN THE OLD TESTAMENT

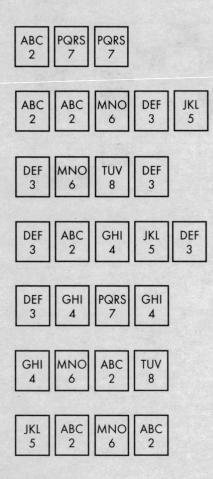

| ABC 2 | PQRS 7 | PQRS 7 |

| ABC 2 | ABC 2 | MNO 6 | DEF 3 | JKL 5 |

| DEF 3 | MNO 6 | TUV 8 | DEF 3 |

| DEF 3 | ABC 2 | GHI 4 | JKL 5 | DEF 3 |

| DEF 3 | GHI 4 | PQRS 7 | GHI 4 |

| GHI 4 | MNO 6 | ABC 2 | TUV 8 |

| JKL 5 | ABC 2 | MNO 6 | ABC 2 |

Day 44

1. DORSW

2. LATEX

3. GONAM

4. RATTESC

5. SAPKE

6. THERSTC

7. NIRU

8. SIRERV

A blind man was given sight in this city.

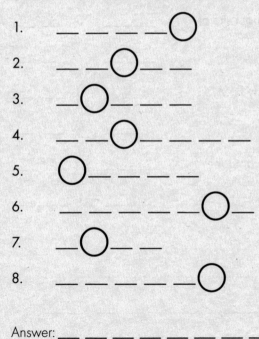

1. __ __ __ __◯

2. __ __◯__ __

3. __◯__ __ __

4. __ __◯__ __ __ __

5. ◯__ __ __ __

6. __ __ __ __ __◯__

7. __◯__ __

8. __ __ __ __ __◯

Answer: __ __ __ __ __ __ __ __

Micah

SAWBILL	Herb	_____	1. ___ ___
HOLIDAY	Circadian	_____	2. ___ ___
ROASTER	Put away	_____	3. ___ ___
TRIPLED	Danger	_____	4. ___ ___
DRESDEN	Thick-headed	_____	5. ___ ___
EPISODE	Caught site of	_____	6. ___ ___
QUENTIN	Boredom	_____	7. ___ ___
HUMERUS	Body fluid	_____	8. ___ ___
ASEPTIC	Room	_____	9. ___ ___
HARDEST	Advantage	_____	10. ___ ___
ENABLED	Dull	_____	11. ___ ___

— — — — — — — — — — —

— — — — — — — — — — —

1 2 3 4 5 6 7 8 9 10 11

Day 46

1 Timothy 4:12

	1	2	3	4	5
1	A	K	E	L	T
2	N	H	F	J	U
3	I	Y	B	X	G
4	O	S	M	D	W
5	R	C	Q	V	P

14-13-15   21-41   43-11-21   44-13-42-55-31-42-13

15-22-32   32-41-25-15-22;   33-25-15   33-13   15-22-41-25

11-21   13-34-11-43-55-14-13   41-23   15-22-13

33-13-14-31-13-54-13-51-42,   31-21   45-41-51-44,

31-21   52-41-21-54-13-51-42-11-15-31-41-21,   31-21

52-22-11-51-31-15-32,   31-21   42-55-31-51-31-15,   31-21

23-11-31-15-22,   31-21   55-25-51-31-15-32.

1 CORINTHIANS 14:10

The parts of a garment that cover the arm

__ __ __ __ __ __ __
38 20 26 8 1 37 14

Not a definite yes or no

__ __ __ __ __
25 30 9 4 21

Blood relatives

__ __ __ __ __ __
36 5 15 32 10 24

Injured unjustly

__ __ __ __ __ __ __
35 13 22 18 3 34 28

To have great depth from side to side

__ __ __ __ __
2 17 12 7 29

Made a coherent whole

__ __ __ __ __ __ __
31 16 6 27 23 11 19

2-17-26-13-21   5-13-8,   12-2   25-5-9   4-11,   14-22

15-5-18-24   29-32-16-19-14

22-36   1-22-12-7-34-14   32-16   2-17-21

35-22-13-10-28,   30-18-28   16-22-18-37

22-36   2-17-34-25   12-38   35-32-2-17-22-31-2

14-6-3-16-32-36-12-7-30-2-32-22-16.

1. ANRE
2. EGNER
3. EIGES
4. SRRUEL
5. SGERLID
6. ESRITS

7. NDOEIRSI
8. NCOIANT
9. RSECATT
10. TPIY
11. UHSOE
12. NAEHEHT

What is it that all believers will experience?

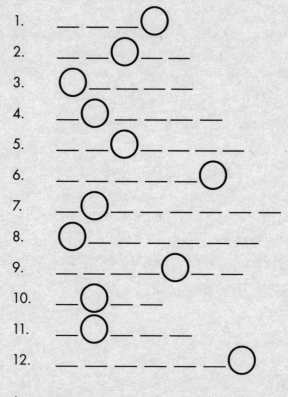

1. __ __ __◯
2. __ __◯__ __
3. ◯__ __ __ __
4. __◯__ __ __ __
5. __ __◯__ __ __ __
6. __ __ __ __◯__
7. __◯__ __ __ __ __
8. ◯__ __ __ __ __ __
9. __ __ __ __◯__ __
10. __◯__ __
11. __◯__ __ __
12. __ __ __ __ __◯

Answer: __ __ __ __ __ __ __ __ __ __ __ __

1. JXZQP   UX   JR   IR   JPD   LGWW;
   KRH   JPRV   ZHJ   UD   BRI: JPD
   OSGHGJ   GO   BRRI;   WXZI   UX
   GYJR   JPX   WZYI   RK
   VSHGBPJYXOO.

2. VUS   BWS   AYVZZ   LQGK   VLVC
   VZZ   RKVMA   XMWD   RYKQM
   KCKA;   VUS   RYKMK   AYVZZ   NK
   UW   DWMK   SKVRY,   UKQRYKM
   AWMMWL,   UWM   FMCQUB,
   UKQRYKM   AYVZZ   RYKMK   NK   VUC
   DWMK   GVQU: XWM   RYK   XWMDKM
   RYQUBA   VMK   GVAAKS   VLVC.

3. MV   EXDPMF   ZUM   VGES   VLLSDSN
   FV   QSUD   FXS   MPGM   VL   TUGH;
   UGN   KGFV   FXST   FXUF   AVVW
   LVD   XPT   MXUAA   XS   URRSUD
   FXS   MSEVGN   FPTS   ZPFXVKF   MPG
   KGFV   MUABUFPVG.

Day 50

OLD TESTAMENT HEADLINES

1.

**COUⱤAGEOUⱤ QUEEN OUⱤWITS
ⱤATEFUL PLOTTING ENEMY**

— — — — — —

2.

**MOTHER RETURNS HOⱤE
AFTER YEⱤRS OF AⱤGUⱤSH**

— — — — — —

3.

**WⱤRRIOR CROSSES ⱤORDAN,
CONQⱤERS LAND, AND
ⱤLAYS PREVIOUS INⱤABITANTS**

— — — — — —

**Day
51**

Isaiah 59:1

```
B   E   H   O   L   D   E   H   A   E
H   I   T   R   E   N   I   A   I   N
N   E   A   S   I   T   H   T   V   R
E   T   H   T   S   A   V   E   H   S
D   N   N   R   E   R   E   T   A   S
H   O   R   A   D   S   O   D   A   N
A   A   T   O   T   N      C   S   Y
    O   T   H   T   H      E      C
    L   O       T         H      T
        I                 H      N
```

Offerings

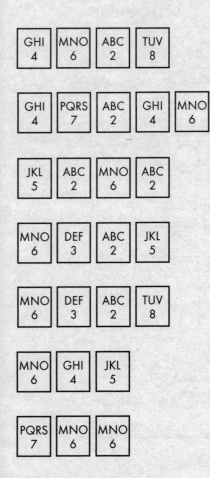

GHI 4	MNO 6	ABC 2	TUV 8	

| GHI 4 | PQRS 7 | ABC 2 | GHI 4 | MNO 6 |

| JKL 5 | ABC 2 | MNO 6 | ABC 2 | |

| MNO 6 | DEF 3 | ABC 2 | JKL 5 | |

| MNO 6 | DEF 3 | ABC 2 | TUV 8 | |

| MNO 6 | GHI 4 | JKL 5 | | |

| PQRS 7 | MNO 6 | MNO 6 | | |

Scrambled Circles

1. NAROFEP
2. TORNERISF
3. YLROG
4. HEAHNET
5. LATESTY

6. SONEB
7. CIVEO
8. MUBD
9. PORPHYSE

A person is made this way because of Christ's sacrifice on the cross.

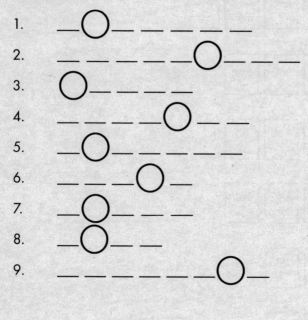

1. __ ⃝ __ __ __ __ __
2. __ __ __ __ __ ⃝ __ __ __
3. ⃝ __ __ __ __
4. __ __ __ __ ⃝ __ __
5. __ ⃝ __ __ __ __ __
6. __ __ __ ⃝ __
7. __ ⃝ __ __ __
8. __ ⃝ __ __
9. __ __ __ __ __ ⃝ __

Answer: __ __ __ __ __ __ __ __ __ __ __

Day 54

Drop Two

DANIEL

LANTERN	Memorize	_____	1. ___ ___
HOLIEST	Shoulder covering	_____	2. ___ ___
ENDWISE	Weaves	_____	3. ___ ___
KESTREL	Oak and maple	_____	4. ___ ___
AMIABLE	Easy walk	_____	5. ___ ___
GRANTED	Scored	_____	6. ___ ___
GURGLED	Stuck	_____	7. ___ ___
MENACED	Beat	_____	8. ___ ___
ABALONE	Aristocrat	_____	9. ___ ___
BLASTED	Apathetic	_____	10. ___ ___
MACHINE	Dishes	_____	11. ___ ___
INVADES	Grape plants	_____	12. ___ ___
AVENGER	Brink	_____	13. ___ ___

1 2 3 4 5 6 7 8 9 10 11 12 13

Day 55

Colossians 3:23

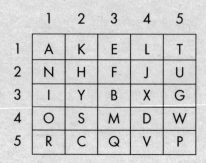

11-21-44   45-22-11-15-42-41-13-54-13-51   32-13

44-41,   44-41   31-15   22-13-11-51-15-31-14-32,

11-42   15-41   15-22-13   14-41-51-44,   11-21-44

21-41-15   25-21-15-41   43-13-21.

1 CORINTHIANS 6:20

A tongue of fire

<u>31</u> <u>38</u> <u>5</u> <u>17</u> <u>9</u>

Not old

<u>39</u> <u>18</u> <u>12</u> <u>3</u> <u>33</u>

The state whose capital is Madison

<u>24</u> <u>28</u> <u>8</u> <u>32</u> <u>21</u> <u>37</u> <u>13</u> <u>35</u> <u>29</u>

An account of a person's life written by another

<u>20</u> <u>34</u> <u>2</u> <u>26</u> <u>23</u> <u>42</u> <u>11</u> <u>16</u> <u>7</u>

An exaggerated picture of a person

<u>10</u> <u>30</u> <u>1</u> <u>22</u> <u>14</u> <u>6</u> <u>36</u> <u>27</u> <u>19</u> <u>41</u>

What a person eats and drinks

<u>15</u> <u>40</u> <u>4</u> <u>25</u>

31-18-23   39-41   6-1-41   20-21-12-33-16-36

24-40-25-16   5   11-23-28-32-9:

25-16-41-23-4-31-2-1-4   33-38-2-23-40-31-7

26-2-15   35-29   7-18-27-23   20-2-15-39,

42-3-15   28-37   39-2-12-19   13-11-34-23-22-36,

24-16-34-10-16   5-19-41   26-2-15'-8.

Scrambled Circles

1. DLEBSES
2. RIPSIT
3. UNORM
4. DFAOBRE
5. LPEINCAN

He threw a party for Jesus but was not prepared for the woman with the perfume.

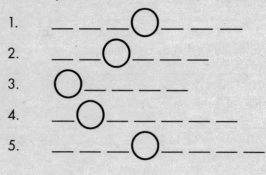

1. __ __ __ ◯ __ __ __
2. __ __ ◯ __ __ __
3. ◯ __ __ __ __
4. __ ◯ __ __ __ __ __
5. __ __ __ ◯ __ __ __ __

Answer: __ __ __ __ __

1. ZXQ QWNQ SWHRW YXPQW
   HZQX QWP UXBQW JPAHDPQW
   N UNZ; FBQ QWNQ SWHRW
   RXUPQW XBQ XA QWP UXBQW,
   QWHK JPAHDPQW N UNZ.

2. NQIWI FH ZAZI QAXM TH NQI
   XAWG: SAW NQIWI FH ZAZI
   OIHFGI NQII: ZIFNQIW FH
   NQIWI TZM WAYD XFDI ACW
   BAG.

3. AX CZI A HAEE NDWATG KAT
   HZDI, AX CZI A KWBG NOJ RL
   JDOTJ; A HAEE XZJ UGWD
   HKWJ UEGTK MWX IZ OXJZ RG.

Old Testament Headlines

1.

**SHEPHERD TRICKED ●Y ●N
UN●UST UN●LE'S PROMISE**

— — — — — —

2.

**BROTHER ●ELLS BIRTHRIGHT
IN RET●RN FOR A M●●L**

— — — — —

3.

**MAN'S WIFE
BEC●MES SA●T S●ATUE**

— — —

**Day
60**

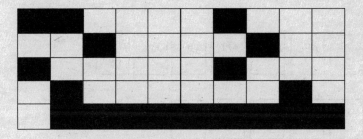

```
L    T    B    E    F    U    E    S    N    D
S    O    T    H    A    V    R    G    H    O    M
E         T    H    O    R         E    O    M    A
          H    E    O
```

Telephone Scrambles

Conversions in the Old Testament

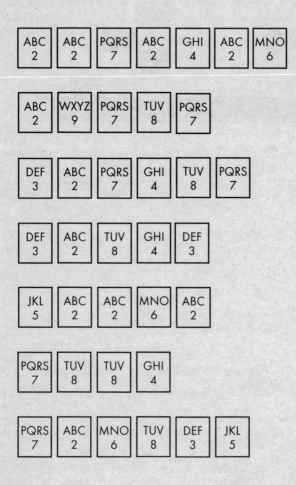

| ABC 2 | ABC 2 | PQRS 7 | ABC 2 | GHI 4 | ABC 2 | MNO 6 |

| ABC 2 | WXYZ 9 | PQRS 7 | TUV 8 | PQRS 7 |

| DEF 3 | ABC 2 | PQRS 7 | GHI 4 | TUV 8 | PQRS 7 |

| DEF 3 | ABC 2 | TUV 8 | GHI 4 | DEF 3 |

| JKL 5 | ABC 2 | ABC 2 | MNO 6 | ABC 2 |

| PQRS 7 | TUV 8 | TUV 8 | GHI 4 |

| PQRS 7 | ABC 2 | MNO 6 | TUV 8 | DEF 3 | JKL 5 |

Scrambled Circles

1. SHLEF
2. NARENM
3. LETAD
4. HISERP
5. TECUXEE
6. NALELF
7. CHRETST
8. RIDEES
9. TIDEESP
10. RUNOM
11. DASHEW

Paul was kept under arrest for two years by these two Roman governors.

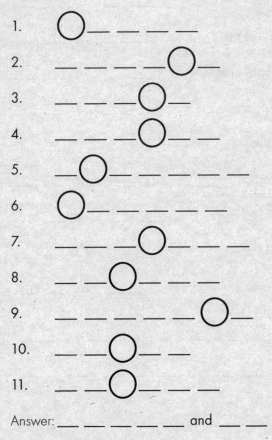

Answer: __ __ __ __ __ __ and __ __ __ __ __ __ __

Day
63

Drop Two

1 SAMUEL

HABITAT	Tropical grass	_____	1.	__ __
PHAROAH	TV hostess	_____	2.	__ __
SKILLET	Cultivates	_____	3.	__ __
LARDING	Wonderful	_____	4.	__ __
TONGUES	Visitor	_____	5.	__ __
MONGREL	Citrus fruit	_____	6.	__ __
THORIDE	Plural pronoun	_____	7.	__ __
SHRIVEL	Angers	_____	8.	__ __
CRUSADE	Whey	_____	9.	__ __
RECEIPT	Portion	_____	10.	__ __
DEATHLY	Doled out	_____	11.	__ __
ONWARDS	Sketched	_____	12.	__ __
PASTEUR	Fastener	_____	13.	__ __

__ __ __ __ __ __ __ __ __ __ __ __ __

__ __ __ __ __ __ __ __ __ __ __ __ __

1 2 3 4 5 6 7 8 9 10 11 12 13

Day 64

Romans 12:19

	1	2	3	4	5
1	A	K	E	L	T
2	N	H	F	J	U
3	I	Y	B	X	G
4	O	S	M	D	W
5	R	C	Q	V	P

44-13-11-51-14-32   33-13-14-41-54-13-44,

11-54-13-21-35-13   21-41-15

32-41-25-51-42-13-14-54-13-42,   33-25-15

51-11-15-22-13-51   35-31-54-13   55-14-11-52-13

25-21-15-41   45-51-11-15-22:   23-41-51   31-15   31-42

45-51-31-15-15-13-21,   54-13-21-35-13-11-21-52-13

31-42   43-31-21-13;   31   45-31-14-14   51-13-55-11-32,

42-11-31-15-22   15-22-13   14-41-51-44.

Acrostic

1 CORINTHIANS 3:17

A set of stairs between floors

$\overline{14}$ $\overline{25}$ $\overline{37}$ $\overline{3}$ $\overline{20}$ $\overline{7}$

Sunrise to sunset

$\overline{24}$ $\overline{8}$ $\overline{30}$ $\overline{26}$ $\overline{19}$ $\overline{2}$ $\overline{13}$

To see something beforehand

$\overline{34}$ $\overline{23}$ $\overline{43}$ $\overline{31}$ $\overline{39}$ $\overline{4}$ $\overline{18}$

An alternate name

$\overline{38}$ $\overline{27}$ $\overline{40}$ $\overline{10}$ $\overline{33}$ $\overline{28}$ $\overline{16}$ $\overline{5}$ $\overline{22}$

A critical study or examination

$\overline{9}$ $\overline{35}$ $\overline{1}$ $\overline{29}$ $\overline{15}$ $\overline{41}$ $\overline{21}$ $\overline{11}$

A male chicken

$\overline{44}$ $\overline{12}$ $\overline{32}$ $\overline{42}$ $\overline{6}$ $\overline{17}$ $\overline{36}$

37-14   8-16-5   22-8-16   24-43-14-41-25-13

15-20-40   7-4-2-34-25-17   12-14   3-32-33,   20-41-22

9-20-8-25-25   3-28-33   24-13-27-15-23-28-11;   14-28-36

6-20-43   26-40-22-34-25-43   28-14   3-12-24

39-27   20-32-25-30,   18-20-41-35-20

7-40-2-38-25-40   30-13   8-1-13.

Scrambled Circles

1. LREEVI
2. EGAELIL
3. ETLEPM
4. YCROTUN
5. ELNGA
6. DEHRA
7. ERCOJIE
8. DROHE
9. NROPSI
10. ELRPA
11. DBEAL

Who is like the greatest in heaven?

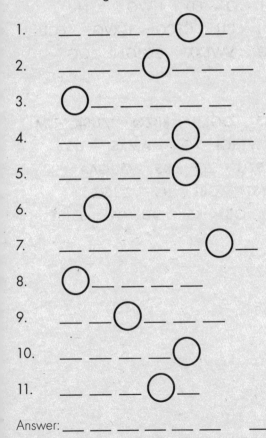

1. __ __ __ __ ◯ __

2. __ __ __ ◯ __ __ __

3. ◯ __ __ __ __ __

4. __ __ __ ◯ __ __

5. __ __ __ ◯

6. __ ◯ __ __ __

7. __ __ __ __ __ ◯ __

8. ◯ __ __ __ __

9. __ __ ◯ __ __ __

10. __ __ __ ◯

11. __ __ __ ◯ __

Answer: __ __ __ __ __ __ __   __ __ __ __ __

1. VTRZBW QP GOSOQUVBD, TEG
   IOTBUM QP RTQE: IBU T FZNTE
   UATU VOTWOUA UAO DZWG,
   PAO PATDD IO CWTQPOG.

2. ECU SG VWEXX RCTL HWEH O
   ED OC HWG DOUVH TY OVNEGX,
   ECU HWEH O ED HWG XTNU
   STPN KTU, ECU CTCG GXVG: ECU
   DS AGTAXG VWEXX CGJGN QG
   EVWEDGU.

3. GBI CSORO OGMI RBZQ ZUSK, M
   GK ZUS WTSGI QX AMXS: US
   ZUGZ EQKSZU ZQ KS OUGAA
   BSJST URBYST; GBI US ZUGZ
   WSAMSJSZU QB KS OUGAA BSJST
   ZUMTOZ.

Old Testament Headlines

1.

**CONNIVING MOTH●R
●NOWINGLY H●LPED SON LIE
TO F●T●ER FO● ●LESSING**

— — — — — — — —

2.

**GOVERNMENT OFF●CI●L
SPEN●S ●IGHT WITH ●IONS**

— — — — — — —

3.

**●EALOUS ●ING
BUILDS ●UGE W●TER TUNNELS
UNDERN●AT● B●S●EGED CITY**

— — — — — — — —

**Day
69**

Psalm 145:1

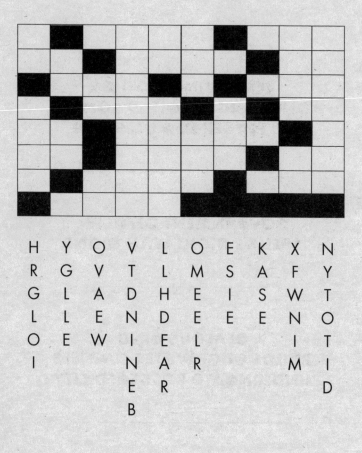

H	Y	O	V		L	O	E	K	X	N
R	G	V	T		L	M	S	A	F	Y
G	L	A	D		H	E	I	S	W	T
L	L	E	N		D	E	E	E	N	O
O	E	W	I		E	L			I	T
I			N		A	R			M	I
			E		R					D
			B							

Day 70

OLD TESTAMENT PLACES

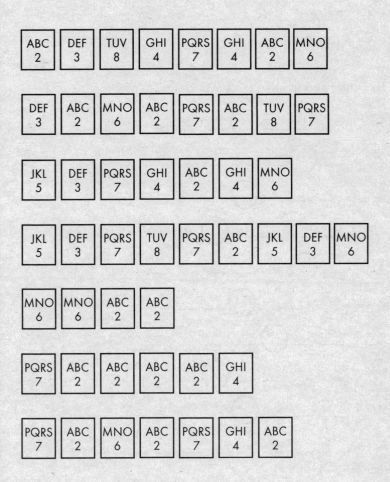

1. BETODR
2. TEBGE
3. CRABHN
4. SITDM
5. NITENEM
6. ROWADT
7. KANET
8. KREBON
9. OPOR

This trade was learned by Jewish boys.

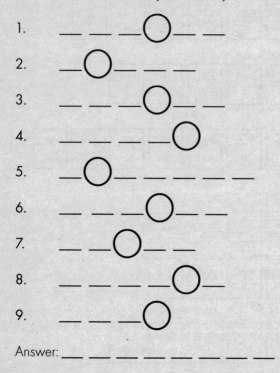

1. __ __ __ O __ __
2. __ O __ __ __
3. __ __ __ O __ __
4. __ __ __ __ __ O
5. __ O __ __ __ __ __
6. __ __ __ O __ __
7. __ __ O __ __
8. __ __ __ __ O __
9. __ __ __ O

Answer: __ __ __ __ __ __ __ __ __

Day 72

2 CHRONICLES

SOMEHOW	Elk	_____	1. ___ ___
HOSPICE	Range	_____	2. ___ ___
SEAPORT	To talk meaninglessly	_____	3. ___ ___
RICHEST	English county	_____	4. ___ ___
HATEFUL	Musical instrument	_____	5. ___ ___
COUNTRY	Woo	_____	6. ___ ___
JUNIPER	Accustom	_____	7. ___ ___
STATURE	Begin	_____	8. ___ ___
DECODED	Granted	_____	9. ___ ___
GRAPHIC	Dept. head	_____	10. ___ ___
ELLIPSE	Heaps	_____	11. ___ ___
CLIMATE	Assert	_____	12. ___ ___

__ __ __ __ __ __ __ __ __ __ __ __

__ __ __ __ __ __ __ __ __ __ __

1 2 3 4 5 6 7 8 9 10 11 12

Psalm 27:1

	1	2	3	4	5
1	T	L	E	K	A
2	U	J	F	H	N
3	G	Z	B	Y	I
4	W	D	M	S	O
5	P	V	Q	C	R

11-24-13   12-45-55-42   35-44   43-34   12-35-31-24-11

15-25-42   43-34   44-15-12-52-15-11-35-45-25;

41-24-45-43   44-24-15-12-12   35   23-13-15-55?

11-24-13   12-45-55-42   35-44   11-24-13

44-11-55-13-25-31-11-24   45-23   43-34   12-35-23-13;

45-23   41-24-45-43   44-24-15-12-12   35   33-13

15-23-55-15-35-42?

PHILIPPIANS 2:14

Continuance of time

___ ___ ___ ___ ___ ___ ___ ___
7 18 13 34 4 39 27 20

Another word for trash

___ ___ ___ ___ ___ ___ ___
31 5 40 23 19 11 17

Unruly and illegal

___ ___ ___ ___ ___ ___ ___
37 12 35 30 42 24 6

Something to be imitated or modeled

___ ___ ___ ___ ___ ___ ___
21 43 32 14 28 1 9

To prove the truth of something

___ ___ ___ ___ ___ ___ ___
8 38 3 22 15 33 26

Agreeable music sounds

___ ___ ___ ___ ___ ___ ___
2 36 25 41 29 16 10

7-38   12-37-1   4-2-15-3-31-24   35-39-4-2-29-18-4

41-18-40-14-18-13-15-16-31-6   32-20-7

7-15-24-28-18-4-39-20-11-6.

Scrambled Circles

1. SJEUS
2. SDLEMA
3. RDPEAT
4. MITE
5. ECVIEER
6. HRONO
7. MKOIDNG

Many feet meant a dramatic change for this place.

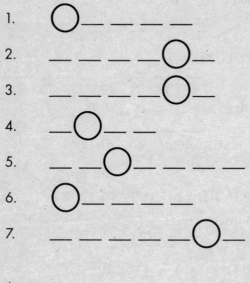

1. ◯ __ __ __ __

2. __ __ __ __◯ __

3. __ __ __ __◯ __

4. __◯ __ __

5. __ __◯ __ __ __ __

6. ◯ __ __ __ __

7. __ __ __ __ __◯ __

Answer: __ __ __ __ __ __ __

1. GWU SYPX EN MYYX, O
   NGPYFM WYSX EF GWU XOI YH
   GPYVKSU; OFX WU JFYLUGW GWUC
   GWOG GPVNG EF WEC.

2. AZC EY FYQQHDC FYUUHEPFXCPYE
   DQYFZZK YHC YG OYHQ UYHCV,
   RHC CVXC JVPFV PL TYYK CY
   CVZ HLZ YG ZKPGOPET, CVXC
   PC UXO UPEPLCZQ TQXFZ HECY
   CVZ VZXQZQL.

3. GVD DUS OHIMHTDST, BUKOU KN
   DUS UHYX CUHND, BUHI DUS
   MQDUST BKYY NSPE KP IX PQIS,
   US NUQYY DSQOU XHV QYY
   DUKPCN, QPE GTKPC QYY DUKPCN
   DH XHVT TSISIGTQPOS,
   BUQDNHSLST K UQLS NQKE
   VPDH XHV.

Old Testament Headlines

1.

**WEALTHIEST ●AN IS A●S●
W●RLD'● M●ST WISE KI●G**

— — — — — — —

2.

**●GYPTIAN FUGITIVE BECO●E●
GOD'S CHO●EN LEADER**

— — — — —

3.

**AUTHOR OF
TEN COMMAN●MENTS
EN●RAVES THEM IN ST●NE**

— — —

JOHN 6:47

```
E   E   R   I   A   Y   S   V   E   V
I   L   Y   H   T   T   O   A   Y   R
M   N   T   A   A   H   H   U   E   H
E   E   L   E   S   T   I   B   N   L
I   E   F   O   L   T       O   E
V   R   T   H   I   Y       N   G
L   I   V   E
U
```

GOD KNOWS OUR. . .

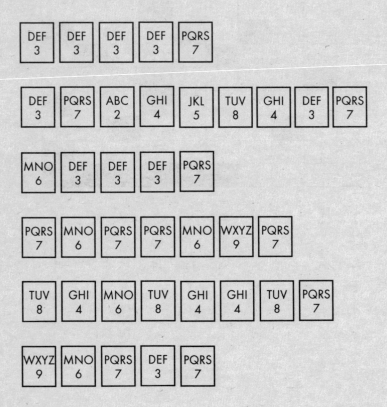

| DEF 3 | DEF 3 | DEF 3 | DEF 3 | PQRS 7 | | | | |

| DEF 3 | PQRS 7 | ABC 2 | GHI 4 | JKL 5 | TUV 8 | GHI 4 | DEF 3 | PQRS 7 |

| MNO 6 | DEF 3 | DEF 3 | DEF 3 | PQRS 7 | | | | |

| PQRS 7 | MNO 6 | PQRS 7 | PQRS 7 | MNO 6 | WXYZ 9 | PQRS 7 | | |

| TUV 8 | GHI 4 | MNO 6 | TUV 8 | GHI 4 | GHI 4 | TUV 8 | PQRS 7 | |

| WXYZ 9 | MNO 6 | PQRS 7 | DEF 3 | PQRS 7 | | | | |

1. NAMEIF
2. DRUNE
3. NATUT
4. TINYNE
5. ROUNYCT
6. HGIH
7. STETTUSA
8. GISEE

Paul's long preaching caused this person to fall out of a window.

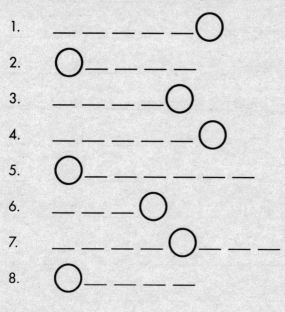

1. __ __ __ __ __◯

2. ◯__ __ __ __

3. __ __ __ __◯

4. __ __ __ __◯

5. ◯__ __ __ __ __ __

6. __ __ __◯

7. __ __ __ __◯__ __ __

8. ◯__ __ __ __

Answer: __ __ __ __ __ __ __ __

NEHEMIAH

WIDOWER	Eerie	_____	1. __ __
FRIGHTS	Hominy	_____	2. __ __
GRAVELY	Bolero composer	_____	3. __ __
RAVIOLI	Competitor	_____	4. __ __
SMASHED	Disgrace	_____	5. __ __
TRIFLED	Angry	_____	6. __ __
HEROISM	Skinflint	_____	7. __ __
READILY	Regularly	_____	8. __ __
HIGHEST	Octave	_____	9. __ __
ADENOSE	Stupid	_____	10. __ __
DUSKIER	Removes wet	_____	11. __ __
SLACKEN	Ringing sound	_____	12. __ __
ENDLESS	Sleighs	_____	13. __ __

__ __ __ __ __ __ __ __ __ __ __ __ __

__ __ __ __ __ __ __ __ __ __ __ __ __

1   2   3   4   5   6   7   8   9   10   11   12   13

Day 82

Romans 14:8

	1	2	3	4	5
1	T	L	E	K	A
2	U	J	F	H	N
3	G	Z	B	Y	I
4	W	D	M	S	O
5	P	V	Q	C	R

23-45-55   41-24-13-11-24-13-55   41-13   12-35-52-13,

41-13   12-35-52-13   21-25-11-45   11-24-13

12-45-55-42;   15-25-42   41-24-13-11-24-13-55   41-13

42-35-13,   41-13   42-35-13   21-25-11-45   11-24-13

12-45-55-42:   41-24-13-11-24-13-55   41-13

12-35-52-13   11-24-13-55-13-23-45-55-13,   45-55

42-35-13,   41-13   15-55-13   11-24-13   12-45-55-42'44.

Psalm 23:6

Fear of being in a confined place

| 6 | 45 | 13 | 28 | 21 | 47 | 26 | 7 | 43 | 34 | 11 | 39 | 20 | 4 |

Faulty

| 14 | 46 | 35 | 5 | 44 | 22 | 42 | 12 | 27 |

The month after April

| 15 | 41 | 29 |

A person who indulges in too much food

| 16 | 30 | 9 | 37 | 19 | 33 | 3 |

To go over something

| 8 | 31 | 24 | 36 | 1 | 17 |

The second story

| 2 | 38 | 10 | 23 | 32 | 40 | 25 | 18 |

21-28-26-46-30-29   16-33-11-14-3-31-18-10

13-3-14   15-46-25-44-29   21-34-13-45-30

35-33-30-45-11-17   15-46   32-30-45   22-34-46

14-4-29-21   11-35   15-29   30-20-35-27:

41-3-14   42   17-40-45-30   14-17-5-45-30   36-3

19-34-27   34-11-9-21-27   11-35

23-34-27   30-33-25-14   35-11-26   1-24-31-8.

Scrambled Circles

1. EPHES
2. CANGNDI
3. EWMNO
4. NNETUIODC
5. PRTUEAC
6. HTENIPSLII

With a little oil, he made David king. Who was he?

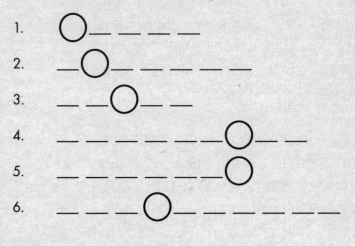

1. ◯_ _ _ _

2. _◯_ _ _ _ _

3. _ _◯_ _

4. _ _ _ _ _ _◯_ _

5. _ _ _ _ _ _◯

6. _ _ _◯_ _ _ _ _ _

Answer: _ _ _ _ _ _

1. DYZ   UB   ILP   LPUNPKB   UZP   LCVLPZ
   ILUK   ILP   PUZIL,   BY   UZP   EX
   RUXB   LCVLPZ   ILUK   XYWZ   RUXB,
   UKT   EX   ILYWVLIB   ILUK   XYWZ
   ILYWVLIB.

2. MNSWS   HNQVV   GYM   QGK   PQG
   FS   QFVS   MY   HMQGL   FSAYWS
   MNSS   QVV   MNS   LQKH   YA   MNK
   VJAS: QH   J   IQH   IJMN   PYHSH,
   HY   J   IJVV   FS   IJMN   MNSS: J
   IJVV   GYM   AQJV   MNSS,   GYW
   AYWHQDS   MNSS.

3. FRU   TDJI   RKFR   KSSUKJUI   DB
   DTI   OYFD   PU,   VKAXYW,   AUK,   X
   RKCU   TDCUI   FRUU   LXFR   KY
   UCUJTKVFXYW   TDCU: FRUJUBDJU
   LXFR   TDCXYWGXYIYUVV   RKCU   X
   IJKLY   FRUU.

OLD TESTAMENT HEADLINES

1.

PROPHET'S ●OURNEY ●INKED TO FI●RY CHOR●OT RIDE UP TO ●EAVEN

— — — — — —

2.

●UST KING RE●T●RES ●EBREW P●SSOVER TO OR●GINAL SPECIFICATIONS

— — — — — —

3.

●RAFTY ●●URNEYMAN WRESTLES WITH ●NGEL AND LIVES TO TELL A●OUT IT

— — — — —

HABAKKUH 3:18

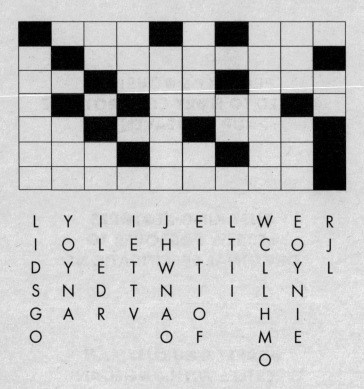

L	Y	I	I	J	E	L	W	E	R
I	O	L	E	H	I	T	C	O	J
D	Y	E	T	W	T	I	L	Y	L
S	N	D	T	N	I	I	L	N	L
G	A	R	V	A	O		H	I	E
O				O	F		M	E	
							O		

Priests

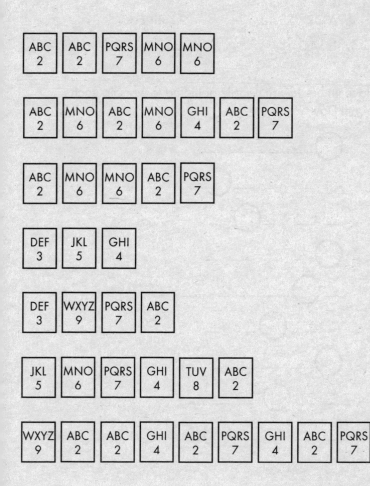

ABC 2	ABC 2	PQRS 7	MNO 6	MNO 6

ABC 2	MNO 6	ABC 2	MNO 6	GHI 4	ABC 2	PQRS 7

ABC 2	MNO 6	MNO 6	ABC 2	PQRS 7

DEF 3	JKL 5	GHI 4

DEF 3	WXYZ 9	PQRS 7	ABC 2

JKL 5	MNO 6	PQRS 7	GHI 4	TUV 8	ABC 2

WXYZ 9	ABC 2	ABC 2	GHI 4	ABC 2	PQRS 7	GHI 4	ABC 2	PQRS 7

Scrambled Circles

1. NOTES
2. MEYEN
3. GONUY
4. RAWOR
5. TAINSAG

6. TOHUS
7. VALREG
8. GOSUHT
9. RIVEUQ

A place where Jewish people gathered to worship each Sabbath Day.

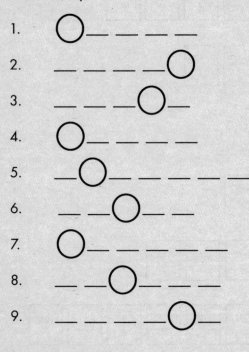

1. ◯ __ __ __ __
2. __ __ __ __ ◯
3. __ __ __ ◯ __
4. ◯ __ __ __ __
5. __ ◯ __ __ __ __
6. __ __ ◯ __ __
7. ◯ __ __ __ __ __
8. __ __ ◯ __ __ __
9. __ __ __ __ ◯ __

Answer: __ __ __ __ __ __ __ __ __

PHILEMON

NEITHER	Triad	_____	1. ___ ___
ASTRIDE	Soils	_____	2. ___ ___
VARSITY	Wander	_____	3. ___ ___
ETHANOL	Reluctant	_____	4. ___ ___
JACINTH	Links	_____	5. ___ ___
HEIRDOM	Entangled	_____	6. ___ ___
EYELASH	Restraint	_____	7. ___ ___
OBELISK	two-wheelers	_____	8. ___ ___
FLOTSAM	Shakes	_____	9. ___ ___
GREATER	Avid	_____	10. ___ ___
DELIGHT	Legal	_____	11. ___ ___

___ ___ ___ ___ ___ ___ ___ ___ ___ ___ ___

___ ___ ___ ___ ___ ___ ___ ___ ___ ___ ___

1   2   3   4   5   6   7   8   9   10   11

Ephisians 4:31

	1	2	3	4	5
1	T	L	E	K	A
2	U	J	F	H	N
3	G	Z	B	Y	I
4	W	D	M	S	O
5	P	V	Q	C	R

12-13-11   15-12-12   33-35-11-11-13-55-25-13-44-44,

15-25-42   41-55-15-11-24,   15-25-42   15-25-31-13-55,

15-25-42   54-12-15-43-45-21-55,   15-25-42

13-52-35-12   44-51-13-15-14-35-25-31,   33-13

51-21-11   15-41-15-34   23-55-45-43   34-45-21,

41-35-11-24   15-12-12   43-15-12-35-54-13.

PROVERBS 22:1

Covered with wet dirt

$\overline{}$ $\overline{}$ $\overline{}$ $\overline{}$ $\overline{}$
12 20 5 17 11

A small green plant with usually three, but sometimes four, leaflets

$\overline{}$ $\overline{}$ $\overline{}$ $\overline{}$ $\overline{}$ $\overline{}$
6 25 21 33 30 8

A male parent

$\overline{}$ $\overline{}$ $\overline{}$ $\overline{}$ $\overline{}$ $\overline{}$
22 29 7 16 26 15

The supposed disembodied spirit of a dead person

$\overline{}$ $\overline{}$ $\overline{}$ $\overline{}$ $\overline{}$
9 31 35 19 2

Not nice

$\overline{}$ $\overline{}$ $\overline{}$ $\overline{}$ $\overline{}$ $\overline{}$ $\overline{}$
10 18 1 13 27 3 24

A person named to receive benefits

$\overline{}$ $\overline{}$ $\overline{}$ $\overline{}$ $\overline{}$ $\overline{}$ $\overline{}$ $\overline{}$ $\overline{}$ $\overline{}$ $\overline{}$
14 28 38 4 37 39 23 40 34 36 32

18   9-35-21-5   10-29-12-26   39-19

36-18-3-27-30-8   3-35   14-4   6-16-21-19-26-38

3-16-29-10   9-36-4-18-3   8-40-23-31-4-19,

18-38-17   25-21-33-40-10-13   22-29-33-21-20-15

36-18-2-27-4-36   7-16-34-10   19-39-25-33-28-36

18-38-17   13-35-25-5.

Scrambled Circles

1. DZINO
2. TBATEL
3. SRINIG
4. BSTERI
5. SPILNA
6. STHTRNEG
7. TCSHOAIR
8. WTODRA
9. EHTDA

This town was home to a widow and her son who were very glad to have Elijah stay with them.

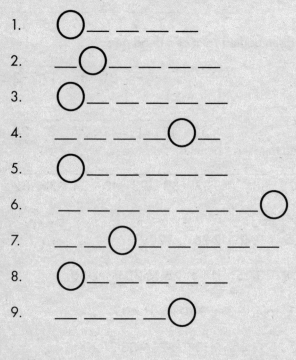

1. ⭘ __ __ __ __
2. __ ⭘ __ __ __ __
3. ⭘ __ __ __ __ __
4. __ __ __ __ ⭘ __
5. ⭘ __ __ __ __ __
6. __ __ __ __ __ __ __ ⭘
7. __ ⭘ __ __ __ __ __
8. ⭘ __ __ __ __ __
9. __ __ __ ⭘

Answer: __ __ __ __ __ __ __ __ __

1. QXKIXGIK HBXQ BI TET
   UKITILCEZYCI, CBIQ BI YNLX
   SYNNIT: YZT HBXQ BI SYNNIT,
   CBIQ BI YNLX FDLCEJEIT: YZT
   HBXQ BI FDLCEJEIT, CBIQ BI
   YNLX ANXKEJEIT.

2. UHN SJKSEESDZ QX ZUF
   EHRQDYIQDODSXX, H YHO!
   ZUSTSWHTS ZUS KUQEOTSD HW
   ASD LVZ ZUSQT ZTVXZ VDOST
   ZUS XUCOHN HW ZUF NQDYX.

3. BAM PYFVFQTQS VYBGG VJQBL
   B PFSM BWBRAVX XYQ VFA FU
   CBA, RX VYBGG EQ UFSWRTQA
   YRC: EZX ZAXF YRC XYBX
   EGBVJYQCQXY BWBRAVX XYQ
   YFGH WYFVX RX VYBGG AFX EQ
   UFSWRTQA.

Old Testament Headlines

1.

WOMAN H●S FI●ST CHILD W●EN ●HE'S ONE HUNDRED YE●RS OLD

— — — — —

2.

BOY ORDERED TO BE S●CRIF●●ED TO TE●T F●THER

— — — — —

3.

UNGODLY KI●G T●ROW● ●●NY CHILDREN INTO FIR●; L●TER REPENT●

— — — — — — — —

Proverbs 15:1

A	E	E	S	W	A	Y	W	A	E
D	S	V	R	O	F	R	R	U	R
S	W	N	S	E	T	T		W	R
I	A	H	G	U	R	T		O	P
T	T		A	T	S	U		N	N
A	H		O	B	I			G	R
H					U				

JUDGES

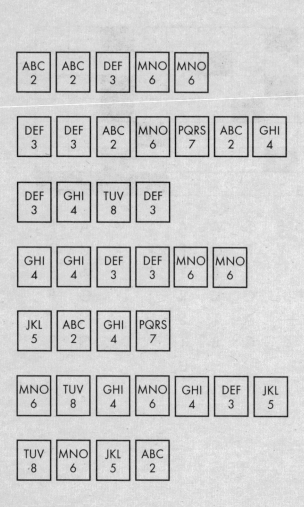

| ABC 2 | ABC 2 | DEF 3 | MNO 6 | MNO 6 |

| DEF 3 | DEF 3 | ABC 2 | MNO 6 | PQRS 7 | ABC 2 | GHI 4 |

| DEF 3 | GHI 4 | TUV 8 | DEF 3 |

| GHI 4 | GHI 4 | DEF 3 | DEF 3 | MNO 6 | MNO 6 |

| JKL 5 | ABC 2 | GHI 4 | PQRS 7 |

| MNO 6 | TUV 8 | GHI 4 | MNO 6 | GHI 4 | DEF 3 | JKL 5 |

| TUV 8 | MNO 6 | JKL 5 | ABC 2 |

1. HASGN
2. TOPEHRP
3. TRECSE
4. DOREVEC
5. RENDUKN
6. YMRIES
7. YDOERST

A kind of magic.

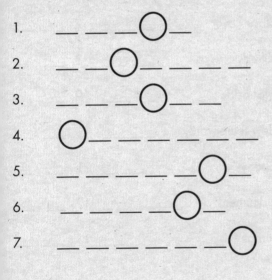

Answer: __ __ __ __ __ __ __

Deuteronomy

LEFTIST	Records	_____	1. __ __
UNHITCH	Overskirt	_____	2. __ __
OPERATE	Chatter	_____	3. __ __
BALEFUL	Legend	_____	4. __ __
EARSHOT	World	_____	5. __ __
COWHERD	Frightened	_____	6. __ __
DETAILS	Floor cover	_____	7. __ __
INSTALL	Killed	_____	8. __ __
SEVENTH	Not odds	_____	9. __ __
BEASTLY	Sew temporarily	_____	10. __ __
BACKLOG	Ebony	_____	11. __ __
APPROVE	Document	_____	12. __ __
PLEASED	Jumps	_____	13. __ __

— — — — — — — — — — — —

— — — — — — — — — — — —

1   2   3   4   5   6   7   8   9   10   11   12   13

Day
100

Matthew 7:8

	1	2	3	4	5
1	T	L	E	K	A
2	U	J	F	H	N
3	G	Z	B	Y	I
4	W	D	M	S	O
5	P	V	Q	C	R

23-45-55   13-52-13-55-34   45-25-13   11-24-15-11

15-44-14-13-11-24   55-13-54-13-35-52-13-11-24;

15-25-42   24-13   11-24-15-11   44-13-13-14-13-11-24

23-35-25-42-13-11-24;   15-25-42   11-45   24-35-43

11-24-15-11   14-25-45-54-14-13-11-24   35-11

44-24-15-12-12   33-13   45-51-13-25-13-42.

Acrostic

PROVERBS 17:28

To disguise for the purpose of blending into the background

__ __ __ __ __ __ __ __ __ __
15 33 8 41 13 36 1 25 20 3

The season that comes after autumn

__ __ __ __ __ __
7 21 14 35 17 2

Number of sides in a pentagon

__ __ __ __
39 22 42 29

Joyful

__ __ __ __ __
4 16 9 19 12

Worship

__ __ __ __ __ __ __ __ __
10 26 31 18 38 6 27 34 23

Lacking energy

__ __ __ __ __ __ __ __
5 32 40 28 11 37 30 24

29-42-37-14   38   39-34-41-1,   7-4-37-23   4-37

4-34-5-26-37-6-4   4-22-24   19-3-10-15-29,   21-30

15-41-13-14-35-29-26   7-32-40-37:   10-14-26   4-17

35-4-33-28   30-4-13-35-6-29-28-4   4-32-40

11-27-9-30   27-24   3-30-35-3-17-8-37-26   33

8-16-23   31-39   13-14-26-3-2-40-6-25-14-26-32-14-20.

1. VAEBO
2. CZRACU
3. TUJNEDGM
4. AWONMRK
5. NIWGILL
6. CEESRIV
7. LBOSW

Wheels and scrolls—a vision for this prophet. Who was he?

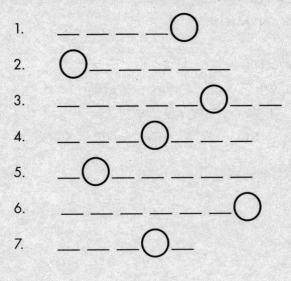

1. __ __ __ __◯

2. ◯__ __ __ __ __

3. __ __ __ __ __◯__ __

4. __ __ __◯__ __ __

5. __◯__ __ __ __ __

6. __ __ __ __ __ __◯

7. __ __ __◯__

Answer: __ __ __ __ __ __ __

1. EGBAB JD EGZE RZNBEG
   GJRDBOC AJVG, PBE GZEG
   YXEGJYF: EGBAB JD EGZE
   RZNBEG GJRDBOC UXXA, PBE
   GZEG FABZE AJVGBD.

2. USC CN BUSC HIVH JSP
   INVMNHI USH KFUUNMK: TGH FL
   VUW ZVU TN V CSMKIFQQNM
   SL JSP, VUP PSNHI IFK CFXX,
   IFZ IN INVMNHI.

3. UOADDAY UA EVY, AIAT FGA
   CSFGAB VC VHB OVBY KADHD
   WGBJDF, FGA CSFGAB VC
   QABWJAD, STY FGA EVY VC SOO
   WVQCVBF.

Old Testament Headlines

1.

**OVER⬤EA⬤OUS QUEEN MURD⬤RS
INNOC⬤NT P⬤OPLE AND
⬤UM⬤LES RELIGION**

— — — — — — —

2.

**SYRI⬤N M⬤N CURED OF
LEPROSY AFTER B⬤THI⬤G
SEVE⬤ TI⬤ES IN RIVER**

— — — — — —

3.

**KING DIES FROM
P⬤INFUL INCU⬤ABLE DIS⬤ASE
AS G⬤D'S ⬤UST PUNIS⬤⬤ENT**

— — — — — — —

Bible Quotation

MATTHEW 11:29

```
O  K  L  K  U  P  M  N  M  E
R  R  A  R  N  D  H  E  A  F
E  T  S  T  N  S  N  Y  E  S
T  K  E  T  D  A  O  N  O  Y
O  U  A  I  A  F  M  E  L  Y
H  A  U  A  E  D  O  E  D  A
L  O     O  F  U  Y  L  O  R
O  N     L     U  M  T     W
R  Y     A           U     S
Y  E     I           L
```

Deacons

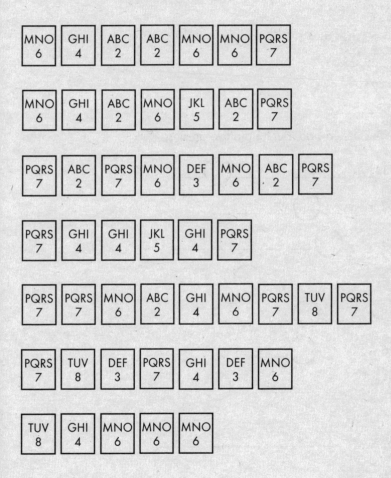

Scrambled Circles

1. DEBOLH
2. HATWC
3. SALZEUO
4. CEPESA
5. KROBO
6. FRUY
7. SHESA

He smelled bad, but he did live again.

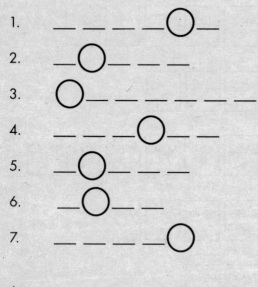

Answer: ___ ___ ___ ___ ___ ___ ___

2 CORINTHIANS

MEDICAL	Sticker	_____	1. ___ ___
CLARIFY	Fragile	_____	2. ___ ___
GLACIER	Understandable	_____	3. ___ ___
PREMIER	Highest grade	_____	4. ___ ___
ANGERED	Avarice	_____	5. ___ ___
CHATTED	Abhorred	_____	6. ___ ___
FEASTED	Help	_____	7. ___ ___
SCORPIO	Marines	_____	8. ___ ___
RESTFUL	Recorder	_____	9. ___ ___
THERMOS	four-base hit	_____	10. ___ ___
UNCOUTH	Nobleman	_____	11. ___ ___
FEARING	Oats	_____	12. ___ ___
FRAGILE	Holy cup	_____	13. ___ ___

__ __ __ __ __ __ __ __ __ __ __ __ __

__ __ __ __ __ __ __ __ __ __ __ __ __

1 2 3 4 5 6 7 8 9 10 11 12 13

JAMES 1:2

	1	2	3	4	5
1	T	L	E	K	A
2	U	J	F	H	N
3	G	Z	B	Y	I
4	W	D	M	S	O
5	P	V	Q	C	R

43-34　33-55-13-11-24-55-13-25,　54-45-21-25-11

35-11　15-12-12　22-45-34　41-24-13-25　34-13

23-15-12-12　35-25-11-45　42-35-52-13-55-44

11-13-43-51-11-15-11-35-45-25-44.

PSALM 1:2

To make something beautiful

__ __ __ __ __ __ __ __
17 40 45 27 7 21 16 37

To repair

__ __ __ __
39 38 5 12

Soaked with fluid

__ __ __ __ __ __ __ __ __ __ __
9 30 2 24 43 20 34 15 44 42 14

Funeral director

__ __ __ __ __ __ __ __ __ __
46 32 11 41 49 23 50 8 4 25

A one hundredth anniversary

__ __ __ __ __ __ __ __ __ __
47 22 48 28 51 10 19 31 1 6

Undecided or doubtful

__ __ __ __ __ __ __ __ __
3 26 35 29 13 18 33 36

17-27-7   3-21-35   11-26-20-29-15-3-2   21-35

31-19   28-3-38   6-50-9   34-16   7-3-22

6-34-25-14;   1-32-11   29-33   3-29-35   20-30-9

12-34-13-3   3-24   39-4-11-21-23-45-13-40

11-18-37   18-48-12   10-29-44-3-36.

Scrambled Circles

1. OBJ
2. EADPPTNOI
3. PRSTOO
4. SRERTOR
5. RISPLAL
6. EBDZEEE
7. TEDXAEL

This is one thing John could do for Jesus.

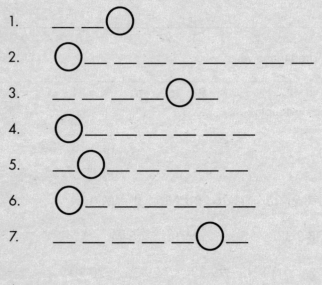

Answer: ___ ___ ___ ___ ___ ___ ___

1. L SLV, GRLF ZIG NB SLV; UZIAB
   DQAA Q HUUO GRUU: NB HLFA
   GRQIHGUGR TLI GRUU, NB
   TAUHR ALMSUGR TLI GRUU QM
   Z VIB ZMV GRQIHGB AZMV,
   DRUIU ML DZGUI QH.

2. DSP GYKLX CSLWW XYD GPLB
   DSLD GSTNS ZPBDLTXPDS EXDY
   L KLX, XPTDSPB CSLWW L KLX
   ZED YX L GYKLX'C RLBKPXD:
   QYB LWW DSLD OY CY LBP
   LMYKTXLDTYX EXDY DSP WYBO
   DSI RYO.

3. WXL NPC HAZL MWQL OXNA
   TAMCM, Q FQHH LA NPQM
   NPQXU WHMA NPWN NPAO PWMN
   MBAGCX: DAZ NPAO PWMN
   DAOXL UZWKC QX TI MQUPN,
   WXL Q GXAF NPCC VI XWTC.

OLD TESTAMENT HEADLINES

1.

**BRAVE ●AN L●ADS THOU●ANDS
ON DRY PATH THROUGH ●EA**

— — — — —

2.

**RIGHTEOUS MAN COPES WITH
SUDDEN L●SS OF
●UST A●OUT EVERYTHING**

— — —

3.

**●AN ●IV●S TO ●EE HIS
NINE H●NDR●D AND
SIX●Y-NINT● BIRT●D●Y**

— — — — — — — — — —

Bible Quotation

Proverbs 2:20

M	Y	Y	N	F	A	H	W	H	L
K	M	I	G	O	H	G	E	U	W
A	E	P	T	H	T	N	O	U	D
T	H	S	E	S	T	E	O	A	K
T	R	A	N	T	F	H	O	P	A
E	H	I	O		T	E	D	O	E
	A	E			T		T		S

Day 115

Telephone Scrambles

Authors

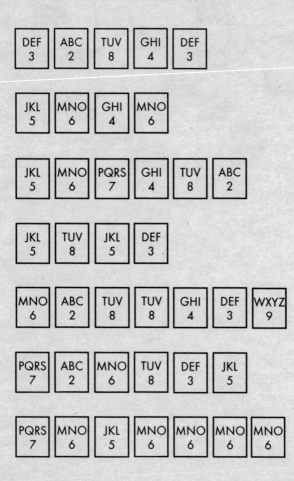

| DEF 3 | ABC 2 | TUV 8 | GHI 4 | DEF 3 | | |

| JKL 5 | MNO 6 | GHI 4 | MNO 6 | | | |

| JKL 5 | MNO 6 | PQRS 7 | GHI 4 | TUV 8 | ABC 2 | |

| JKL 5 | TUV 8 | JKL 5 | DEF 3 | | | |

| MNO 6 | ABC 2 | TUV 8 | TUV 8 | GHI 4 | DEF 3 | WXYZ 9 |

| PQRS 7 | ABC 2 | MNO 6 | TUV 8 | DEF 3 | JKL 5 | |

| PQRS 7 | MNO 6 | JKL 5 | MNO 6 | MNO 6 | MNO 6 | MNO 6 |

Scrambled Circles

1. DGIAEL
2. EVCINOEL
3. EKLIDN
4. POWIRHS
5. ETNER
6. SOFOR
7. TFREAHR
8. EFRI
9. FILE
10. ANLEONB
11. BADIE

Flowers that grow wild all over Galilee.

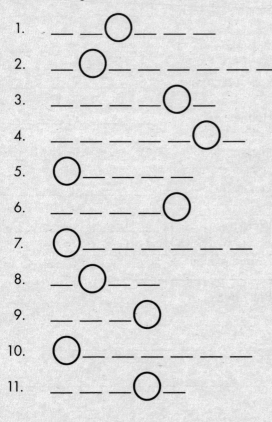

1. __ __ ◯ __ __ __
2. __ ◯ __ __ __ __ __ __
3. __ __ __ __ ◯ __
4. __ __ __ __ __ ◯ __
5. ◯ __ __ __ __
6. __ __ __ __ ◯
7. ◯ __ __ __ __ __ __
8. __ ◯ __ __
9. __ __ __ ◯
10. ◯ __ __ __ __ __ __
11. __ __ __ ◯ __

Answer: __ __ __ __ __ __ of the __ __ __ __ __

Day 117

Drop Two

PHILIPPIANS

ALBANIA	Veranda	_____	1.	__ __
POINTER	Trash	_____	2.	__ __
AVENGER	Novice	_____	3.	__ __
MACHETE	Instruct	_____	4.	__ __
RESPITE	Stumbles	_____	5.	__ __
WHARVES	Apportion	_____	6.	__ __
HAIRNET	Railroad cars	_____	7.	__ __
INDOORS	Hairnet	_____	8.	__ __
CLARIFY	Style	_____	9.	__ __
HANGING	Ripening	_____	10.	__ __
MALARIA	Warning	_____	11.	__ __
FLOTSAM	Parade exhibit	_____	12.	__ __
ASCRIBE	Baby beds	_____	13.	__ __

—— —— —— —— —— —— —— —— —— —— —— —— ——

—— —— —— —— —— —— —— —— —— —— —— —— ——

1   2   3   4   5   6   7   8   9   10   11   12   13

Day 118

Ephesians 6:11

	1	2	3	4	5
1	T	L	E	K	A
2	U	J	F	H	N
3	G	Z	B	Y	I
4	W	D	M	S	O
5	P	V	Q	C	R

51-21-11   45-25   11-24-13   41-24-45-12-13

15-55-43-45-21-55   45-23   31-45-42,   11-24-15-11

34-13   43-15-34   33-13   15-33-12-13   11-45

44-11-15-25-42   15-31-15-35-25-44-11   11-24-13

41-35-12-13-44   45-23   11-24-13   42-13-52-35-12.

MATTHEW 6:6

Confused

___ ___ ___ ___ ___ ___ ___ ___ ___ ___
42 6   23 35 15 30 1   25 19 31

An impediment

___ ___ ___ ___ ___ ___ ___ ___ ___
33 24 14 40 22 4   12 36 9

A dentifrice

___ ___ ___ ___ ___ ___ ___ ___ ___ ___
46 10 27 44 34 5   38 26 17 32

A soft, plastic mixture used to hold things together

___ ___ ___ ___ ___
11 3   20 29 37

A sudden, brief light

___ ___ ___ ___ ___
13 2   21 7   41

The soul

___ ___ ___ ___ ___ ___
45 28 43 8   39 16

42-3-20   44-34-10-3,   23-33-1-14   46-34-27-3

28-8-21-37-1-45-20,   6-12-46-19-25   39-14-16-10

46-34-37   36-15-27-45-1-29,   21-14-40

23-34-32-14   46-34-10-3   41-21-26-17   26-34-3-16

16-41-37   31-27-10-22,   11-22-4-37   17-27

29-41-37   13-38-20-41-9-8   23-33-43-36-34

24-26   35-14   7-6-36-22-19-29.

1. SOECMNU
2. LEXTA
3. AEPELRUS
4. NSTERAV
5. EANRWS
6. RHIOPWS
7. RAUPETS

In the beginning, there was nothing to separate the water, until God created it. What was it (NIV)?

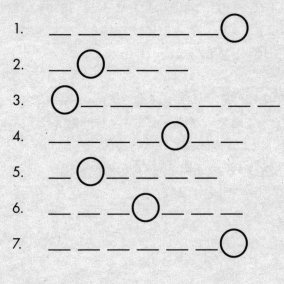

1. __ __ __ __ __ __◯

2. __ ◯__ __ __

3. ◯__ __ __ __ __ __ __

4. __ __ __ __◯__ __

5. __ ◯__ __ __ __

6. __ __ __◯__ __

7. __ __ __ __ __◯

Answer: __ __ __ __ __ __ __

1. GVRXSV ELV CXHQEPYQO BVSV
GSXHDLE RXSEL, XS VWVS ELXH
LPFOE RXSCVF ELV VPSEL PQF
ELV BXSTF, VWVQ RSXC
VWVSTPOEYQD EX VWVSTPOEYQD,
ELXH PSE DXF.

2. CIALZI H JTYYBQ RA BETU HY
ILYRQBR CTOBJ, HYR ITJ RHNJ
WB VQAUAYZBR, NBC JLQBUN T
MYAG CIHC TC JIHUU WB GBUU
GTCI CIBO CIHC XBHQ ZAR,
GITKI XBHQ WBXAQB ITO.

3. IJF OBIRWKXPXE MX FK AJ
OKEF KE FXXF, FK ITT AJ RBX
JISX KD RBX TKEF VXWQW,
CAPAJC RBIJUW RK CKF IJF
RBX DIRBXE HM BAS.

OLD TESTAMENT HEADLINES

1.

DIS●BEDIENT PROPHET E●DURES THREE DAYS IN ●UMBO FISH'S STOM●C●

— — — — —

2.

WOMAN'S ●NGUIS●ED PRAYERS ●●SWERED T●ROUGH BIRTH OF SO●

— — — — — —

3.

RIG●TEOUS PRI●ST KILLED BY ●NTENTION●LLY FO●GETFUL KING AND OVER●E●LOUS ●●●●RTS

— — — — — — — — — —

Jude 2

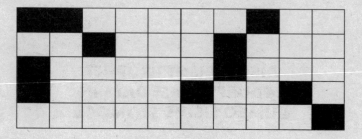

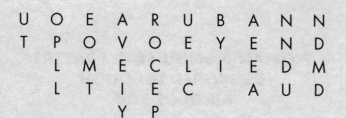

```
U    O    E    A    R    U    B    A    N    N
T    P    O    V    O    E    Y    E    N    D
     L    M    E    C    L    I    E    D    M
     L    T    I    E    C         A    U    D
               Y    P
```

BOOKS OF THE OLD TESTAMENT

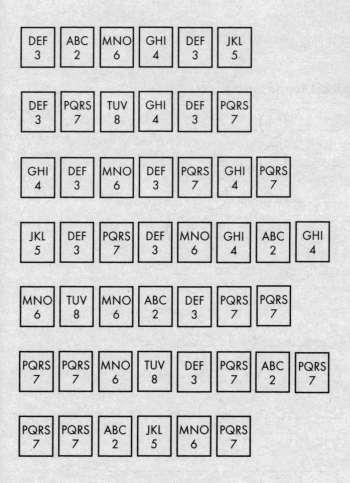

Scrambled Circles

1. EISNNCE
2. DANME
3. NGLAE
4. RTLEVO
5. DUBENR

6. TPRAUER
7. IANTON
8. OWYLHL
9. DFNREI

An important Roman army officer.

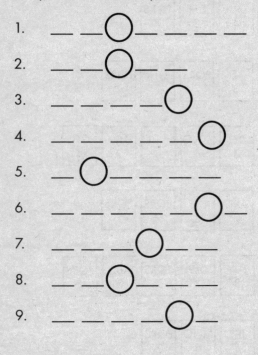

1. __ __ ◯ __ __ __ __ __
2. __ __ ◯ __ __
3. __ __ __ __ ◯
4. __ __ __ __ __ __ ◯
5. __ ◯ __ __ __ __
6. __ __ __ __ ◯ __
7. __ __ __ ◯ __ __
8. __ __ ◯ __ __ __
9. __ __ __ __ ◯ __

Answer: __ __ __ __ __ __ __ __ __

2 THESSALONIANS

HURTLED	Attracted	_____	1. __ __
HEARTEN	Devoured	_____	2. __ __
GREASED	Pulls	_____	3. __ __
RESPOND	Modeled	_____	4. __ __
ENDLESS	Lets borrow	_____	5. __ __
FEASTED	Alleviated	_____	6. __ __
BEGONIA	Commence	_____	7. __ __
FLANKER	Chip	_____	8. __ __
EPISODE	Bearing	_____	9. __ __
FIBSTER	Sacraments	_____	10. __ __
BARRING	Carry	_____	11. __ __
REVISED	Operate vehicle	_____	12. __ __
FLATTER	Signal light	_____	13. __ __

__ __ __ __ __ __ __ __ __ __ __ __ __

__ __ __ __ __ __ __ __ __ __ __ __ __

1 2 3 4 5 6 7 8 9 10 11 12 13

Psalm 4:2

	1	2	3	4	5
1	T	L	E	K	A
2	U	J	F	H	N
3	G	Z	B	Y	I
4	W	D	M	S	O
5	P	V	Q	C	R

45   34-13   44-45-25-44   45-23   43-13-25,

24-45-41   12-45-25-31   41-35-12-12   34-13

11-21-55-25   43-34   31-12-45-55-34   35-25-11-45

44-24-15-43-13?   24-45-41   12-45-25-31   41-35-12-12

34-13   12-45-52-13   52-15-25-35-11-34,   15-25-42

44-13-13-14   15-23-11-13-55   12-13-15-44-35-25-31?

PROVERBS 25:11

A close acquaintance

___ ___ ___ ___ ___ ___
26   3   20 13 33 6

Existing only in one's head

___ ___ ___ ___ ___ ___ ___ ___ ___
12 21 1 34 31 17 28 22 7

An abbreviation for the state of which Salt Lake City
is the capital

___ ___
5   8

A clasp for fastening a strap or belt

___ ___ ___ ___ ___ ___
27 14 29 9 23 32

Wet, marshy land

___ ___ ___ ___ ___
10 24 15 2 19

One who makes or sells gloves

___ ___ ___ ___ ___ ___
4 16 18 30 11 25

15   24-18-22-6   26-12-8-23-7   10-19-18-9-11-33

31-10   23-20-9-11   1-19-19-23-13-10   18-26

4-18-23-6   31-17   19-12-29-8-14-25-13-10   18-26

10-12-16-30-13-3.

Scrambled Circles

1. NAEET
2. EBSON
3. ETLEBRIK
4. RHTHAE
5. SRUIOGEHT
6. EOCRNDAIN
7. YEMEN

This righteous man had a difficult time with fear.

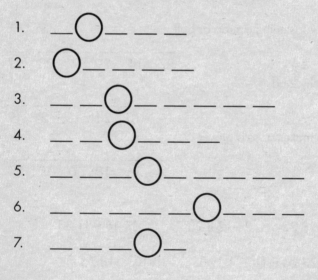

1. __ ◯ __ __ __
2. ◯ __ __ __ __
3. __ __ ◯ __ __ __ __ __
4. __ __ ◯ __ __ __
5. __ __ __ ◯ __ __ __ __
6. __ __ __ __ __ ◯ __ __ __
7. __ __ __ ◯ __

Answer: __ __ __ __ __ __ __

1. BGF RYWP HDYAFBG GYA BY
   PFRTUFW BGF OYPRI YSB YV
   BFLKBMBTYDJ, MDP BY WFJFWUF
   BGF SDNSJB SDBY BGF PMI YV
   NSPOLFDB BY EF KSDTJGFP.

2. QAAS CYFIDAGBAD ZU MJA GYBA
   YX TYL, GYYQZUT XYI MJA
   RAIEC YX YFI GYIL VADFD
   EJIZDM FUMY AMAIUOG GZXA.

3. JKT LHOFO CWWPZKR FBWK
   SEHX OJZSE, MZSE XHK ZS ZO
   ZXBWOOZVCH, VFS KWS MZSE
   RWT: NWI MZSE RWT JCC
   SEZKRO JIH BWOOZVCH.

OLD TESTAMENT HEADLINES

1.

**WOAK MAN SUBOUES
MIOHTY ARMY WOTH ONLY
THREE HUODRED MEN**

— — — — — —

2.

**DAOOLING KIOG OOMOLOD
AND FOROEO TO
EOT GOOSS LIKO OXEO**

— — — — — — — — — — — —

3.

**GOO CHOOSES
SONGING SHEPHERO TO
BECOME FOOORED KING**

— — — — —

**Day
132**

Psalm 76:4

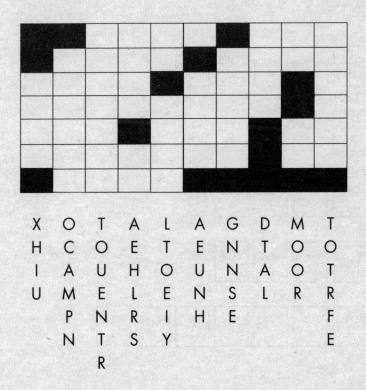

```
X   O   T   A   L   A   G   D   M   T
H   C   O   E   T   E   N   T   O   O
I   A   U   H   O   U   N   A   O   T
U   M   E   L   U   N   S   L   R   R
    P   N   R   I   H   E       R   F
    N   T   S   Y   H       E       E
        R
```

FOODS IN THE NEW TESTAMENT

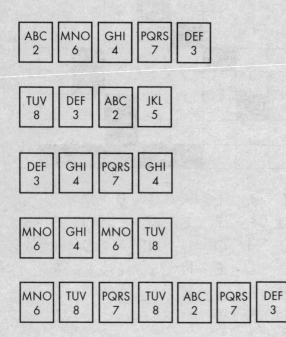

| ABC 2 | MNO 6 | GHI 4 | PQRS 7 | DEF 3 |

| TUV 8 | DEF 3 | ABC 2 | JKL 5 |

| DEF 3 | GHI 4 | PQRS 7 | GHI 4 |

| MNO 6 | GHI 4 | MNO 6 | TUV 8 |

| MNO 6 | TUV 8 | PQRS 7 | TUV 8 | ABC 2 | PQRS 7 | DEF 3 |

Scrambled Circles

1. DLOBO
2. ODWIW
3. REWAS
4. SDTU
5. SYFLALE
6. NSDTA

7. SACEU
8. YGPLNIA
9. LEPEPO
10. EECEUTX
11. URODN

A celebration to help us remember all that the Lord has done for us.

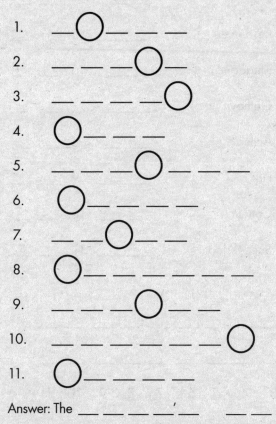

1. ___ ⭕ ___ ___ ___
2. ___ ___ ___ ⭕ ___
3. ___ ___ ___ ___ ⭕
4. ⭕ ___ ___ ___
5. ___ ___ ___ ⭕ ___ ___ ___
6. ⭕ ___ ___ ___ ___
7. ___ ___ ⭕ ___ ___
8. ⭕ ___ ___ ___ ___ ___ ___
9. ___ ___ ___ ⭕ ___ ___
10. ___ ___ ___ ___ ___ ⭕
11. ⭕ ___ ___ ___ ___

Answer: The ___ ___ ___ ___ ' ___   ___ ___ ___ ___ ___ ___

PROVERBS

GARFISH	Expositions	_____	1. ___ ___
ORATION	Educate	_____	2. ___ ___
TROUPER	Cowboy	_____	3. ___ ___
SUCROSE	Oath	_____	4. ___ ___
MANTLES	Resources	_____	5. ___ ___
HUMERAL	Kingdom	_____	6. ___ ___
GRAINED	Outflow	_____	7. ___ ___
GOADING	Acting	_____	8. ___ ___
ALCORAN	Pink	_____	9. ___ ___
GREATER	Concur	_____	10. ___ ___
DRAFTED	Succeeded	_____	11. ___ ___

__ __ __ __ __ __ __ __ __ __ __

__ __ __ __ __ __ __ __ __ __ __

 1   2   3   4   5   6   7   8   9   10 11

Day
136

1 CORINTHIANS 10:14

	1	2	3	4	5
1	T	L	E	K	A
2	U	J	F	H	N
3	G	Z	B	Y	I
4	W	D	M	S	O
5	P	V	Q	C	R

41-24-13-55-13-23-45-55-13,   43-34

42-13-15-55-12-34   33-13-12-45-52-13-42,

23-12-13-13   23-55-45-43   35-42-45-12-15-11-55-34.

Psalm 12:6

To be involved in

‗ ‗ ‗ ‗ ‗ ‗ ‗ ‗ ‗ ‗ ‗
16 38 26 17 36 48 1 43 9 34 24

An exciting undertaking

‗ ‗ ‗ ‗ ‗ ‗ ‗ ‗ ‗
47 3 37 44 18 25 2 49 12

Perfect

‗ ‗ ‗ ‗ ‗ ‗ ‗ ‗
19 46 27 13 42 8 40 33

To grumble

‗ ‗ ‗ ‗ ‗ ‗
29 35 10 28 5 20

The real thing

‗ ‗ ‗ ‗ ‗ ‗ ‗ ‗ ‗
4 22 31 11 45 14 7 21 39

Directed forward

‗ ‗ ‗ ‗ ‗ ‗
15 30 32 41 23 6

17-11-8   13-15-26-3-40   15-19   7-11-44

42-15-49-3   41-20-5   43-35-20-8   32-15-49-3-33:

9-40   40-1-46-37-12-49   25-23-21-45-6   36-14   27

19-2-49-30-4-39-45   15-19   24-38-20-31-11,

16-22-26-21-19-36-8-6   33-5-37-8-18

10-21-29-8-40.

1. HJAEIRME

2. OTERULB

3. KSAPE

4. RNHEEIT

5. DBLUI

6. HTSAIRSH

This son of Nun took control of a nation.

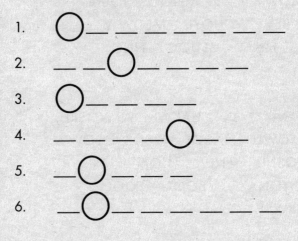

1. ◯— — — — — — — —

2. — —◯— — — —

3. ◯— — — —

4. — — — —◯— —

5. —◯— — —

6. —◯— — — — — —

Answer: __ __ __ __ __ __

1. DM DJ NZZS MUKM K PKQ
   JUZEHS YZMU UZRF KQS
   LEDFMHV CKDM XZA MUF
   JKHTKMDZQ ZX MUF HZAS.

2. RNY BEC IOV NR BEC WNYI
   UM QCOY JZNQ OWW BEC
   ECOBECQ: OM BENJ EOMB INQC,
   UB MEOWW LC INQC JQBN
   BECC: BEV YCHOYI MEOWW
   YCBJYQ JZNQ BEUQC NHQ
   ECOI.

3. RSM FOAX AX HAKW WFWNSRH,
   FORF FOWU TACOF VSQB FOWW
   FOW QSHU FNLW CQM, RSM
   IWXLX YONAXF, BOQT FOQL
   ORXF XWSF.

Old Testament Headlines

1.

INNOCEN● LA●D●WNER MURDERED FOR ●IS ●E●UTIFUL PLOT OF LAND

— — — — — —

2.

M●N'S DONKEY ST●RTS SCO●DING HI● IN HE●REW LANGU●GE

— — — — — —

3.

●EALOUS EX-CAPTIVE T●ACES LIN●AGE BACK TO HIGH PRIEST ●ARON

— — — —

Day
141

Luke 14:11

```
D    F    O    A    H    W    X    H    S    O
H    V    E    E    A    E    M    S    L    T
I    T    H    B    L    I    L    A    E    L
E    U    S    R    E    L    E    O    H    A
E    M    D    H    S    E    H    A    A    L
F    L    B    R    L    T    D    X    A    L
L    A    H    E    L    E    H    S    T    E
T    E    S    B    B    F    T    S    B    N
     S    M                            H    H
```

Moutains

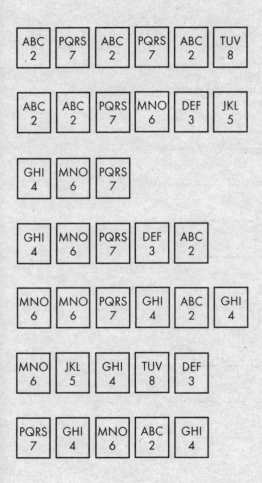

| ABC 2 | PQRS 7 | ABC 2 | PQRS 7 | ABC 2 | TUV 8 |

| ABC 2 | ABC 2 | PQRS 7 | MNO 6 | DEF 3 | JKL 5 |

| GHI 4 | MNO 6 | PQRS 7 |

| GHI 4 | MNO 6 | PQRS 7 | DEF 3 | ABC 2 |

| MNO 6 | MNO 6 | PQRS 7 | GHI 4 | ABC 2 | GHI 4 |

| MNO 6 | JKL 5 | GHI 4 | TUV 8 | DEF 3 |

| PQRS 7 | GHI 4 | MNO 6 | ABC 2 | GHI 4 |

Scrambled Circles

1. SHTTRI
2. WSSRHEO
3. IEASR
4. NPLTA
5. WYAA
6. RJECET
7. EORPRSP
8. NAGHEC
9. NGKIS

It was because of this that Paul ended up on the island of Melita.

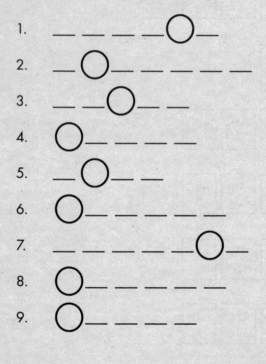

1. __ __ __ __ ◯ __
2. __ ◯ __ __ __ __ __
3. __ __ ◯ __ __
4. ◯ __ __ __ __
5. __ ◯ __ __
6. ◯ __ __ __ __ __
7. __ __ __ __ ◯ __
8. ◯ __ __ __ __
9. ◯ __ __ __ __

Answer: __ __ __ __ __ __ __ __ __ __

ECCLESIASTES

CLOTHES	Nearby	_____	1. __ __
OPALINE	Not fancy	_____	2. __ __
DECLARE	Tied shoes	_____	3. __ __
REVOLVE	Sweetheart	_____	4. __ __
CEILING	Adhere	_____	5. __ __
DESSERT	Horse	_____	6. __ __
ANALYST	Diagonal	_____	7. __ __
STALEST	Slightest	_____	8. __ __
INSHORE	Found in varnish	_____	9. __ __
ALGERIA	Royal	_____	10. __ __
SINGLED	Move smoothly	_____	11. __ __
GUNSHOT	Shift	_____	12. __ __
INSTANT	Discolor	_____	13. __ __

__ __ __ __ __ __ __ __ __ __ __ __ __

__ __ __ __ __ __ __ __ __ __ __ __ __

1 2 3 4 5 6 7 8 9 10 11 12 13

Day
145

Psalm 24:9

	1	2	3	4	5
1	T	U	G	W	P
2	L	J	Z	D	V
3	E	F	B	M	Q
4	K	H	Y	S	C
5	A	N	I	O	R

21-53-32-11   12-15   43-54-12-55   42-31-51-24-44,

54   43-31   13-51-11-31-44;   31-25-31-52

21-53-32-11   11-42-31-34   12-15,   43-31

31-25-31-55-21-51-44-11-53-52-13   24-54-54-55-44;

51-52-24   11-42-31   41-53-52-13   54-32

13-21-54-55-43   44-42-51-21-21   45-54-34-31

53-52.

COLOSSIANS 3:16

An elected official

___ ___ ___ ___ ___ ___ ___ ___ ___ ___
6 29 11 37 27 40 34 3 17 22

To twist and whirl

___ ___ ___ ___ ___
18 4 15 10 36

Word endings that sound alike

___ ___ ___ ___ ___
30 16 26 5 38

A container for restaurant leftovers

___ ___ ___ ___ ___ ___ ___ ___ ___
12 28 7 21 32 2 13 23 35

To rotate

___ ___ ___ ___
1 8 14 24

To fail to remember

___ ___ ___ ___ ___ ___
25 9 33 20 39 31

36-38-27   1-16-39   4-28-30-12   9-25

34-16-30-37-18-31   12-4-2-11-36   32-24   26-29-8

10-15-34-16-11-26   40-22   17-36-11

4-40-18-12-9-5;   27-39-17-34-16-32-24-7   23-22-12

17-12-5-29-22-3-18-16-3-24-20   29-24-39   17-22-28-1-16-2-30

40-22   6-18-17-36-5-18   17-22-12   16-26-5-24-18

23-22-12   18-6-37-14-15-31-8-17-11   18-28-24-35-18.

Scrambled Circles

1. SWSIELNDRE
2. YCROTUN
3. TWHAE
4. TWHEGI
5. RMEREMEB
6. RLDO
7. EBTRALEC
8. OZNI

This couple fell in love on a threshing floor.

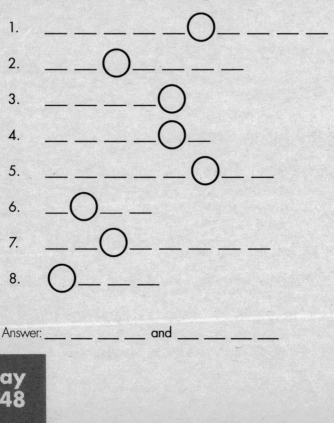

1. __ __ __ __ Ⓞ __ __ __ __
2. __ Ⓞ __ __ __ __
3. __ __ __ Ⓞ
4. __ __ __ Ⓞ __
5. __ __ __ __ Ⓞ __ __
6. Ⓞ __ __
7. __ Ⓞ __ __ __ __ __
8. Ⓞ __ __ __

Answer: __ __ __ __ and __ __ __ __

CryptoScriptures

1. W UPRTYN NRUYUATYU, NRDN, AWYJN TA DII, JLBBIWMDNWTCJ, BYDHUYJ, WCNUYMUJJWTCJ, DCK ZWFWCZ TA NRDCOJ, QU GDKU ATY DII GUC.

2. CRTFQRY, JFTTFG WFK KPLK GPNSP NX RQNT, CDK KPLK GPNSP NX EFFY. PR KPLK YFRKP EFFY NX FJ EFY: CDK PR KPLK YFRKP RQNT PLKP WFK XRRW EFY.

3. TNO JQI ONP NT JQI HUDXIP EQKFF SNJ OIEJ MWNS JQI FNJ NT JQI OUBQJINME; FIEJ JQI OUBQJINME WMJ TNOJQ JQIUO QKSPE MSJN USYMUJR.

OLD TESTAMENT HEADLINES

1.

EX-SPY RE●EIV●S PORTION OF ●EAUTIFUL PROMISED ●●ND

— — — — —

2.

IMMORA● WOMAN TRICKS JU●GE ●NTO REVE●●ING S●CRET STRENGT●

— — — — —

3.

MAN TW●CE CHALLE●●ES GOD TO ●EWDR●P T●STS

— — — — — —

Hebrews 13:8

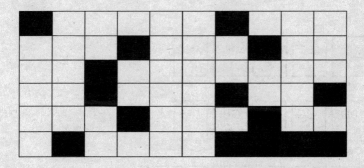

```
M   E   Y   Y   U   S   E   T   O   O
A   Y   E   A   T   D   T   C   F   A
D   A   T   S   E   N   D   E   S   D
I   J   E   V   N   S       R   R
R   S       N   S           H
            A   H
            E   R
```

People of the Old Testament

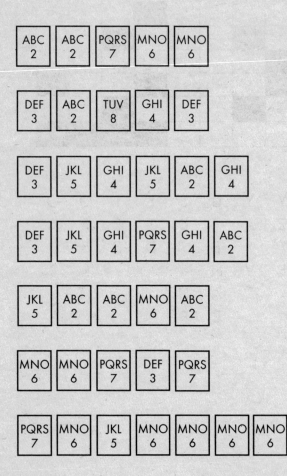

| ABC 2 | ABC 2 | PQRS 7 | MNO 6 | MNO 6 |

| DEF 3 | ABC 2 | TUV 8 | GHI 4 | DEF 3 |

| DEF 3 | JKL 5 | GHI 4 | JKL 5 | ABC 2 | GHI 4 |

| DEF 3 | JKL 5 | GHI 4 | PQRS 7 | GHI 4 | ABC 2 |

| JKL 5 | ABC 2 | ABC 2 | MNO 6 | ABC 2 |

| MNO 6 | MNO 6 | PQRS 7 | DEF 3 | PQRS 7 |

| PQRS 7 | MNO 6 | JKL 5 | MNO 6 | MNO 6 | MNO 6 | MNO 6 |

1. NTPROOI
2. YAMRR
3. EGRTOF
4. UBTEAY
5. EREMREMB
6. LPSERKNI
7. FRIEG

A story that theaches a lesson.

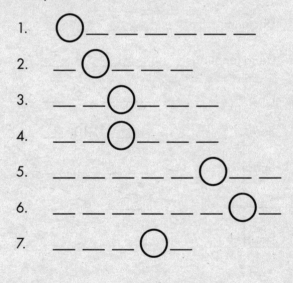

1. 〇__ __ __ __ __ __
2. __ 〇__ __ __
3. __ __ 〇__ __ __
4. __ __ 〇__ __ __
5. __ __ __ __ __ 〇__ __
6. __ __ __ __ __ __ 〇__
7. __ __ __ 〇__

Answer: __ __ __ __ __ __ __

Drop Two

PSALMS

FITMENT	Pretense	_____	1. __ __
HONESTY	Rock	_____	2. __ __
HOSTILE	Panel part	_____	3. __ __
USHERED	Tear into strips	_____	4. __ __
AGAINST	Bite	_____	5. __ __
FINLAND	Last	_____	6. __ __
COWERED	Doctrine	_____	7. __ __
INITIAL	Dead language	_____	8. __ __
CHASTEN	Pursue	_____	9. __ __
FREIGHT	Sorrow	_____	10. __ __
TROUBLE	Speak out	_____	11. __ __
CESSION	Breakfast roll	_____	12. __ __
SCARLET	Frighten	_____	13. __ __

__ __ __ __ __ __ __ __ __ __ __ __ __

__ __ __ __ __ __ __ __ __ __ __ __ __

1 2 3 4 5 6 7 8 9 10 11 12 13

Decoder

1 Corinthians 9:22

	1	2	3	4	5
1	T	U	G	W	P
2	L	J	Z	D	V
3	E	F	B	M	Q
4	K	H	Y	S	C
5	A	N	I	O	R

11-54 11-42-31 14-31-51-41 33-31-45-51-34-31

53 51-44 14-31-51-41, 11-42-51-11 53

34-53-13-42-11 13-51-53-52 11-42-31 14-31-51-41:

53 51-34 34-51-24-31 51-21-21 11-42-53-52-13-44

11-54 51-21-21 34-31-52, 11-42-51-11 53

34-53-13-42-11 33-43 51-21-21 34-31-51-52-44

44-51-25-31 44-54-34-31.

PSALM 13:6

Jekyll and. . .

$\overline{\quad}_{30} \ \overline{\quad}_{4} \ \overline{\quad}_{18} \ \overline{\quad}_{9}$

To struggle with something

$\overline{\quad}_{17} \ \overline{\quad}_{8} \ \overline{\quad}_{24} \ \overline{\quad}_{3} \ \overline{\quad}_{32} \ \overline{\quad}_{15} \ \overline{\quad}_{11}$

A bison

$\overline{\quad}_{25} \ \overline{\quad}_{16} \ \overline{\quad}_{26} \ \overline{\quad}_{5} \ \overline{\quad}_{35} \ \overline{\quad}_{23} \ \overline{\quad}_{31}$

Humid

$\overline{\quad}_{28} \ \overline{\quad}_{2} \ \overline{\quad}_{10} \ \overline{\quad}_{36} \ \overline{\quad}_{19}$

Relating to times long past

$\overline{\quad}_{14} \ \overline{\quad}_{1} \ \overline{\quad}_{20} \ \overline{\quad}_{12} \ \overline{\quad}_{33} \ \overline{\quad}_{7} \ \overline{\quad}_{27}$

Of herbs

$\overline{\quad}_{6} \ \overline{\quad}_{29} \ \overline{\quad}_{22} \ \overline{\quad}_{13} \ \overline{\quad}_{21} \ \overline{\quad}_{34}$

12   17-12-23-15   3-12-1-10   2-1-27-31   27-6-29

34-31-8-18,   13-11-20-35-16-3-11   30-33

6-14-32-30   18-9-21-23-27

25-31-16-7-27-12-5-16-15-34-4   17-12-27-6   28-24.

1. AGTRE

2. EHOSSR

3. SLJUEOA

4. DTIMS

5. MJEELRAUS

6. TPELMUM

7. SHTOS

He should have ducked. Who was he?

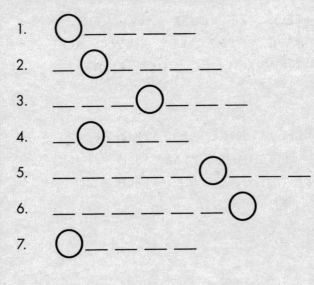

1. ○ __ __ __ __

2. __ ○ __ __ __ __

3. __ __ __ ○ __ __ __

4. __ ○ __ __ __

5. __ __ __ __ __ ○ __ __ __

6. __ __ __ __ __ __ ○

7. ○ __ __ __ __

Answer: __ __ __ __ __ __ __

1. JLU WV GLX D FDG, XQDX QR
   VQLBKU KWR; GRWXQRS XQR
   VLG LE FDG, XQDX QR VQLBKU
   SRARGX: QDXQ QR VDWU, DGU
   VQDKK QR GLX UL WX? LS
   QDXQ QR VALPRG, DGU VQDKK
   QR GLX FDPR WX JLLU?

2. SWK RENY LWUYK KLWYWZEYW
   DW TWYZWJK BQKL KLW SEYO
   ENY FEO, KE BUSX QV LQC
   CKUKNKWC, UVO KE XWWT LQC
   JEAAUVOAWVKC, UC UK KLQC
   OUR.

3. PU KZPQJ JQJLE HJ ZBQFGE,
   FPOJ ZPL HGJNC KD JNK; NQC
   PU ZJ HJ KZPGVKE, FPOJ ZPL
   INKJG KD CGPQA.

Old Testament Headlines

1.

**WOMAN DRIVES
WOODEN P●G ●UST THROUGH
S●EEPING ENEMY'S HE●D**

— — — —

2.

**RUL●R PU●●LED ●Y
MY●TE●IOUS ●●ND WRITING
ON THE W●L●**

— — — — — — — — — — —

3.

**●ABITUALLY STUBBORN
EGY●TI●N ●ULER ●ASN'T LET
GOD'S PE●PLE LE●VE**

— — — — — — —

JAMES 1:8

```
M   I   S   D   O   D   S   T   E   B
H   E   N   I   E   N   A   L   A   N
L   A   S   D   U   U   B   L   L
    I       N   A   Y   S   A
    I       W       M
```

HEAVEN IS A PLACE OF...

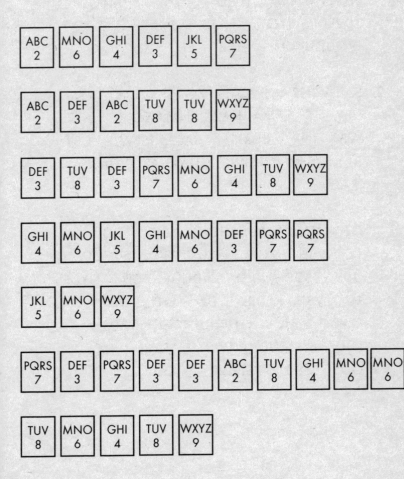

1. HKB   WJB   UHBY   MDY   LVQUHUYKM,
   HKB   BVIVBYB   MDY   XHMYQG
   XDVPD   XYQY   CKBYQ   MDY
   LVQUHUYKM   LQJU   MDY   XHMYQG
   XDVPD   XYQY   HRJIY   MDY
   LVQUHUYKM: HKB   VM   XHG   GJ.

2. SAL   INR   JWQY   ZGRU: SAL   RYSM
   USY   S   FMAAHAZ   NMAIRG,   S   PSA
   WB   INR   BHRXL;   SAL   TSFWJ   USY
   S   KXSHA   PSA,   LURXXHAZ   HA
   IRAIY.

3. GE   VBDL   PUDFHEV   UDV   FBGV
   TE   VBH   FGM   DX   VBH   EQTYTV,
   UDY   BDF   VBH   NDUHE   SD   OYDF
   TU   VBH   FDJN   DX   BHY   VBGV   TE
   FTVB   ABTCS: HRHU   ED   VBDL
   PUDFHEV   UDV   VBH   FDYPE   DX
   ODS   FBD   JGPHVB   GCC.

Ephesians

Word	Clue		#	
CHARITY	Dept. head	_____	1.	___ ___
HEADMAN	Titled	_____	2.	___ ___
SMARTEN	Streetcars	_____	3.	___ ___
BLADDER	Leaf of grass	_____	4.	___ ___
ELEANOR	Find out	_____	5.	___ ___
GENTIAN	Representative	_____	6.	___ ___
RICKETS	Magic	_____	7.	___ ___
OVERSAW	Vacillate	_____	8.	___ ___
PARSNIP	French capital	_____	9.	___ ___
EROSIVE	Left-hand page	_____	10.	___ ___
GRABBER	Flat-bottom boat	_____	11.	___ ___
OPALINE	Woodworking tool	_____	12.	___ ___
REDDEST	Woodwinds	_____	13.	___ ___

__ __ __ __ __ __ __ __ __ __ __ __ __

__ __ __ __ __ __ __ __ __ __ __ __ __

1 2 3 4 5 6 7 8 9 10 11 12 13

Day 163

Psalm 18:3

	1	2	3	4	5
1	T	U	G	W	P
2	L	J	Z	D	V
3	E	F	B	M	Q
4	K	H	Y	S	C
5	A	N	I	O	R

53   14-53-21-21   45-51-21-21   12-15-54-52

11-42-31   21-54-55-24,   14-42-54   53-44

14-54-55-11-42-43   11-54   33-31

15-55-51-53-44-31-24:   44-54

44-42-51-21-21   53   33-31   44-51-25-31-24

32-55-54-34   34-53-52-31   31-52-31-34-53-31-44.

Psalm 8:1

Costly

___ ___ ___ ___ ___ ___ ___ ___ ___
10 44 34 13 26 2   42 20 7

Using correct reasoning

___ ___ ___ ___ ___ ___ ___
24 39 8   35 30 14 18

An onlooker

___ ___ ___ ___ ___ ___ ___ ___ ___
21 25 17 43 36 6   40 19 38

To beg in a childish, undignified way

___ ___ ___ ___ ___
31 3   15 9   27

A signature

___ ___ ___ ___ ___ ___ ___ ___ ___
4   28 47 1   22 45 16 37 11

To hug

___ ___ ___ ___ ___ ___ ___
23 46 5   41 29 12 32

39   24-1-41-40   39-28-38   18-39-45-40,

11-39-31   7-44-30-10-24-18-19-6-43   42-2

43-11-25   26-14-46-23   35-26   29-24-18

47-3-7   19-16-38-43-3!   31-3-1   11-4-17-43

2-23-43   43-3-25   22-24-1-41-25   36-5-1-20-10

43-11-27   3-13-16-20-32-9-2.

Scrambled Circles

1. LSUIFN
2. RFEAHT
3. EALSBSEM
4. NVOISI
5. SGSLEAND

6. NBERHETR
7. HFTAI
8. DOEPEN
9. DFNOU

Whom shall we fear when the Lord is our light and our. . .?

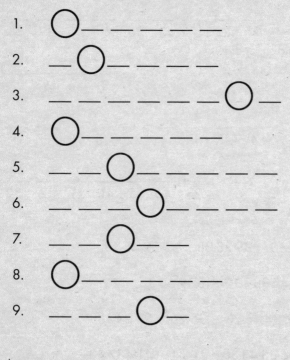

1. ⭕— — — — —
2. — ⭕— — — —
3. — — — — — — ⭕—
4. ⭕— — — —
5. — — ⭕— — — —
6. — — — ⭕— — —
7. — — ⭕— —
8. ⭕— — — —
9. — — — ⭕—

Answer: ___ __ __ __ __ __ __ __ __

1. EGNYKGXY, G XUR QDJT RTQ, JWYCY GX MTR GD JWY ZCYXYDSY TA JWY UDPYEX TA PTI TBYC TDY XGDDYC JWUJ CYZYDJYJW.

2. RCN JQV FHNF PFQXBK NFB OQQYTXF NFTKJX QO NFB GQIYV NQ PQKOQCKV NFB GTXB; HKV JQV FHNF PFQXBK NFB GBHD NFTKJX QO NFB GQIYV NQ PQKOQCKV NFB NFTKJX GFTPF HIB UTJFNZ.

3. RSI BWJ XSLJ SR OSYJN FQ BWJ ISSB SR KXX JLFX: EWFDW EWFXJ QSOJ DSLJBJU KRBJI, BWJN WKLJ JIIJU RISO BWJ RKFBW, KYU CFJIDJU BWJOQJXLJQ BWISGHW EFBW OKYN QSIISEQ.

OLD TESTAMENT HEADLINES

1.

**PROPOET FORETELLS
JESUS' BORTH, DEOTH,
OND REOURRECTOON**

— — — — — —

2.

**MAN'S NEWOY GIVEN NOME TO
OEPREOENT AN ONTORE NATION**

— — — — — —

3.

**WICKED OAN PLOTS TO OANG
QUEEO'S ODOPTED FOTHER**

— — — — — —

**Day
168**

JOB 23:10

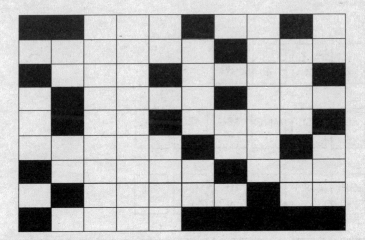

N	G	T	U	T	E	H	T	H	E
N	R	H	E	T	H	M	A	T	S
I	S	I	Y	R	T	H	W	H	K
E	W	B	A	D	T	A	C	A	E
T	O	W	E	D	H	H	E	H	I
	F	E	K	L		T	O	M	
	O	A	L			E			
	A	O							
	H	L							

Cᴜʀsᴇᴅ

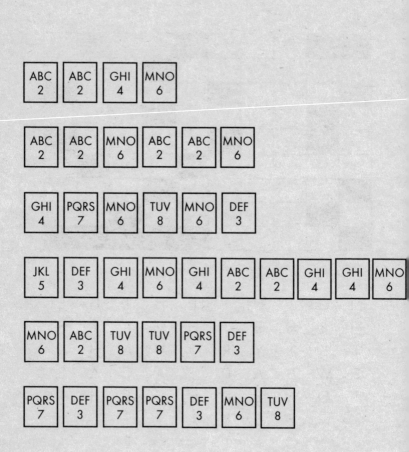

PROVERBS 16:32

Finicky

___ ___ ___ ___ ___
16 36 30 1   9

Took into the stomach

___ ___ ___ ___ ___ ___ ___ ___ ___
39 10 31 15 25 4   21 8   42

A raised area

___ ___ ___ ___
5   26 22 35

To rinse the throat with a liquid, using air from the lungs
to make bubbles

___ ___ ___ ___ ___ ___
12 38 17 2   32 43

A person hired as a driver

___ ___ ___ ___ ___ ___ ___ ___ ___
33 3   11 24 37 7   28 14 18

Nourishing

___ ___ ___ ___ ___ ___ ___ ___ ___ ___
6   20 29 40 19 41 27 34 13 23

3-28   29-3-31-29   36-39   23-32-4-10   29-34

31-6-12-43-17   19-23   5-8-29-41-8-18   29-3-31-6

29-3-8   22-19-2-3-41-9;   31-6-42   3-28   29-3-31-29

17-13-25-43-29-3   3-36-23   39-16-36-40-19-41

29-3-31-6   3-28   41-3-31-29   41-11-1-8-29-3   38

30-27-41-9.

JAMES

Word	Clue		Answer
BLOTCHY	Angrily	_____	1. ___ ___
ARCUATE	Wooden case	_____	2. ___ ___
NASCENT	Weaves	_____	3. ___ ___
NATURAL	Related to hearing	_____	4. ___ ___
HOODING	Performing	_____	5. ___ ___
MARKETS	Bare	_____	6. ___ ___
ASEPTIC	Paprika	_____	7. ___ ___
ORATION	Proportion	_____	8. ___ ___
NOBLEST	Tree trunks	_____	9. ___ ___
AGAINST	Discolor	_____	10. ___ ___
UMPIRED	Self-esteem	_____	11. ___ ___
ESCAPEE	Cloaks	_____	12. ___ ___

__ __ __ __ __ __ __ __ __ __ __ __

__ __ __ __ __ __ __ __ __ __ __ __

1 2 3 4 5 6 7 8 9 10 11 12

Day 172

Proverbs 27:1

	1	2	3	4	5
1	T	U	G	W	P
2	L	J	Z	D	V
3	E	F	B	M	Q
4	K	H	Y	S	C
5	A	N	I	O	R

33-54-51-44-11   52-54-11   11-42-43-44-31-21-32

54-32   11-54-34-54-55-55-54-14;   32-54-55

11-42-54-12   41-52-54-14-31-44-11   52-54-11

14-42-51-11   51   24-51-43   34-51-43

33-55-53-52-13   32-54-55-11-42.

**Day
173**

Bible Quotation

JOHN 14:6

```
H  W     I  Y     I  S     H  T     N  O
R  U     A  H     U  T     N  E     E  T
T  F     B  L     N  M     O  T     B  U
H  J     E  N     H  T     E  D     A  I
T  E     A  T     A  A     M  S     H  I
M  M     U  S     T  F     R  H     I  T
   H     T  U        C     E  H        E
      A     Y  N        O              E
               N        E
                        M
```

1. ASIMAAR
2. ERVEMO
3. ESEPRHUCL
4. DAENTION
5. MBETEHLHE
6. TCNOAVNE
7. NCIAATP

He made the right choice and was blessed more than any other man.

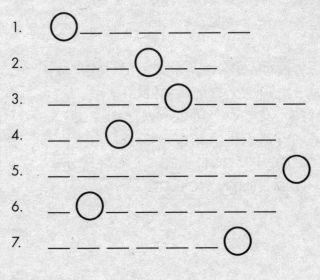

1. ◯ _ _ _ _ _ _
2. _ _ _ ◯ _ _
3. _ _ _ _ ◯ _ _ _ _
4. _ _ ◯ _ _ _ _
5. _ _ _ _ _ _ _ ◯
6. _ ◯ _ _ _ _ _
7. _ _ _ _ _ _ ◯

Answer: _ _ _ _ _ _ _

1. JFMUMXZUM JM UMQMKEKVD S
   YKVDWZI JFKQF QSVVZL OM
   IZEMW, TML RN FSEM DUSQM,
   JFMUMOC JM ISC NMUEM DZW
   SQQMALSOTC JKLF UMEMUMVQM
   SVW DZWTC XMSU.

2. QT JD MQT VPOW, QJD KPVW JD
   ZTVLTOM: LPV YHH QJD KYXD
   YVT FBCARTUM: Y APC PL
   MVBMQ YUC KJMQPBM JUJNBJMX,
   FBDM YUC VJAQM JD QT.

3. GC GRBG IRNC BGC CRYBG EH
   GKM DQVCY, GC GRBG
   CMBREUKMGCN BGC VQYUN EH
   GKM VKMNQI, RTN GRBG
   MBYCBZGCN QOB BGC GCRFCTM
   EH GKM NKMZYCBKQT.

OLD TESTAMENT HEADLINES

1.

**TALKING SNAK●
D●CEI●ES WOMAN**

—— —— ——

2.

**SLUM●ERING MAN IS ●ARRED
WHEN HE ●AN SEE
ST●IRWAY T● HEAVEN IN DREAM**

—— —— —— —— ——

3.

**YO●NG BOY H●●RS
GOD CAL● HIS NA●E
THREE TIME● IN ONE NIGHT**

—— —— —— —— —— ——

**Day
177**

ROMANS 12:17

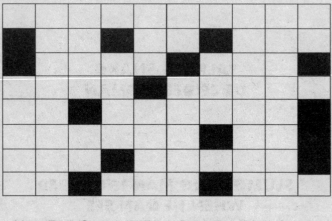

```
H  E  O  L  N  P  F  M  A  N
T  T  V  T  L  I  R  O  R  E
E  E  I  E  S  T  G  O  V  N
O  V  E  O  S  P  E  G  T  I
R  E  C  A  M  O  N  M  E
D  O  N  I  L  L  N  S
   H     I  H  I     I  S
   F        H     H  N
```

Altar Makers

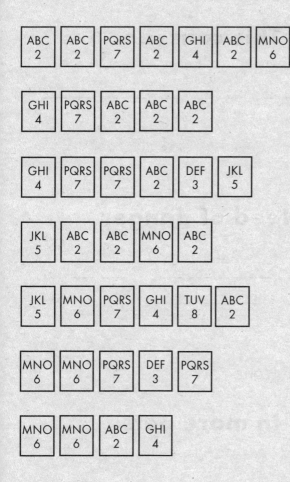

Books of the Bible. . .

This coin ran

— — — — — — — — — — —

Places. . .

Need of danger

— — — — — —   — —
— — — —

New Testament People. . .

In more pets

— — — — —   — — — — —

REVELATION

ANTIQUE	Silent	_____	1. ___ ___
NODDING	Acting	_____	2. ___ ___
AVERAGE	Serious	_____	3. ___ ___
WESTERN	Change	_____	4. ___ ___
HELICES	Pie serving	_____	5. ___ ___
CHOWDER	Musical tones	_____	6. ___ ___
MEDIATE	Measured speed	_____	7. ___ ___
CANVASS	Browses	_____	8. ___ ___
PRELATE	Home base	_____	9. ___ ___
NASTIER	Pay hike	_____	10. ___ ___
SPANISH	Whirls	_____	11. ___ ___

__ __ __ __ __ __ __ __ __ __ __

__ __ __ __ __ __ __ __ __ __ __

1   2   3   4   5   6   7   8   9   10   11

**Day
181**

Psalm 4:8

	1	2	3	4	5
1	T	U	G	W	P
2	L	J	Z	D	V
3	E	F	B	M	Q
4	K	H	Y	S	C
5	A	N	I	O	R

53   14-53-21-21   33-54-11-42   21-51-43   34-31

24-54-14-52   53-52   15-31-51-45-31,   51-52-24

44-21-31-31-15:   32-54-55   11-42-54-12,

21-54-55-24,   54-52-21-43   34-51-41-31-44-11

34-31   24-14-31-21-21   53-52   44-51-32-31-11-43.

Psalm 18:2

A place of secondary education

___ ___ ___ ___   ___ ___ ___ ___ ___ ___
34 5 17 12   1 29 25 16 42 15

The British spelling of "flavor"

___ ___ ___ ___ ___ ___ ___
18 4 32 24 28 45 43

To move around in a twisting motion

___ ___ ___ ___ ___ ___
11 40 37 23 33 8

A record of days, months, and years

___ ___ ___ ___ ___ ___ ___ ___
9 26 13 30 20 41 38 3

The process of returning to health

___ ___ ___ ___ ___ ___ ___ ___
19 6 35 2 21 14 27 44

A location for buying or selling

___ ___ ___ ___ ___ ___
10 31 39 7 36 22

22-34-8   4-28-27-41   40-1   10-44   39-42-35-7,

31-20-41   10-44   18-42-43-22-39-14-1-1,   32-20-41

10-44   41-30-13-5-21-14-39-36-19;   10-44   23-16-41,

10-44   1-22-3-30-20-17-22-12,   40-20

11-25-2-10   5   11-5-13-15   22-39-45-1-22.

Scrambled Circles

1. POCSMAS
2. AEITCVP
3. TSLEDAOE
4. YBBOANL

5. VGLRAE
6. NNSDEPA
7. TTRSIA
8. DHMAESA

Jewish men would meet here to talk and do business.

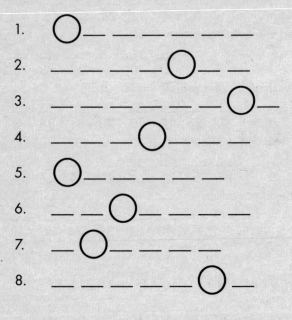

1. ◯ — — — — — —
2. — — — — ◯ — —
3. — — — — — — ◯ —
4. — — — ◯ — — —
5. ◯ — — — — —
6. — — ◯ — — — —
7. — ◯ — — — —
8. — — — — — ◯ —

Answer: __ __ __ __   __ __ __ __

1. LRN AI RHF SHRXHBOIN FH
FTKY JHBWN: AMF AI PI
FBLRYXHBOIN AP FTI BIRIJKRC
HX PHMB OKRN, FTLF PI OLP
QBHDI JTLF KY FTLF CHHN, LRN
LSSIQFLAWI, LRN QIBXISF, JKWW
HX CHN.

2. VJK V HZXRP RVYP ZNE ZI EBP
EBLZJP, WVGXJO, SLVXWP ZNL
OZK, VMM GP BXW WPLHVJEW,
VJK GP EBVE IPVL BXY, DZEB
WYVMM VJK OLPVE.

3. MZC VOCFEZC YUOCF OC OL
OPNELLOMWI CE NWIULI FOP: YEH
FI CFUC DEPICF CE RET PZLC
MIWOIGI CFUC FI OL, UST CFUC
FI OL U HIVUHTIH EY CFIP
CFUC TOWORISCWQ LIIA FOP.

NEW TESTAMENT HEADLINES

1.

**ASTOTE DOCTOR WRITOS
TWO BOOOS OF THE BIBOE**

— — — —

2.

**BABY JESUS MEOTIOOED BY
ELDERLY JERUSALEM
TEMPLE LODY TO OLL**

— — — —

3.

**FAVORITE DISCIPLE
SEES OARRING EOD TIMES
IN OIS VISION**

— — — —

Bible Quotation

HEBREWS 3:15

```
I  S  H  I  L  V  F  E  T  O
A  D  E  S  L  E  H  I  T  E
R  W  I  O  A  R  O  V  Y  R
T  H  A  Y  A  R  D  I  A  C
T  T  I  L  P  E  N  H  C  O
H  I  R  N  I  O  I  N  A
H  Y  S  D  S     I  N  E
T  S  O  U  I        E  E
W  A                 N
                     O
```

Telephone Scrambles

DIVINE REPORTS OF CHRIST'S BIRTH

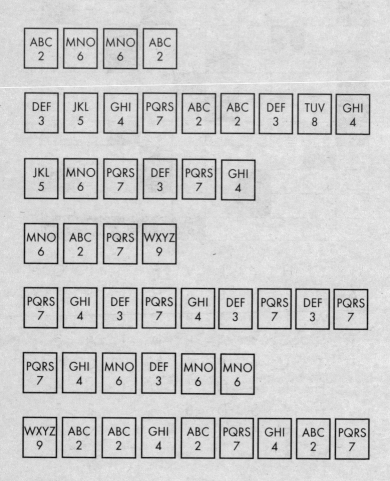

Events. . .

Joe felt choir tab

_ _ _ _ _ _ _   _ _

_ _ _ _ _ _ _

Books of the Bible. . .

See sing

_ _ _ _ _ _ _

Rivers/Bodies of Water. . .

See a dad

_ _ _ _   _ _ _

Drop Two

Ezekiel

BLANKLY	Skinny	_____	1. __ __
LOCATED	Military trainee	_____	2. __ __
PRESENT	Exhausted	_____	3. __ __
SLAVERY	Disentangle	_____	4. __ __
DESPOIL	Heaped	_____	5. __ __
FREAKED	Gathered leaves	_____	6. __ __
TRASHED	Clip sheep	_____	7. __ __
BEARISH	Uplift	_____	8. __ __
BEREAVE	Daring	_____	9. __ __
AILMENT	N.E. state	_____	10. __ __
ALCOHOL	Nearby	_____	11. __ __
BOARDER	Wide	_____	12. __ __
SINGLED	Paper guides	_____	13. __ __

__ __ __ __ __ __ __ __ __ __ __ __ __

__ __ __ __ __ __ __ __ __ __ __ __ __

1 2 3 4 5 6 7 8 9 10 11 12 13

Day 190

1 Corinthians 9:27

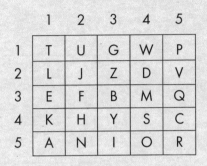

	1	2	3	4	5
1	T	U	G	W	P
2	L	J	Z	D	V
3	E	F	B	M	Q
4	K	H	Y	S	C
5	A	N	I	O	R

33-12-11   53   41-31-31-15   12-52-24-31-55   34-43

33-54-24-43...21-31-44-11   11–42-51-11   33-43

51-52-43   34-31-51-52-44,   14-42-31-52

53   42-51-25-31   15-55-31-51-45-42-31-24   11-54

54-11-42-31-55-44,   53   34-43-44-31-21-32

44-42-54-12-21-24   33-31   51

45-51-44-11-51-14-51-43.

PSALM 2:11

Fairness

$$\overline{33}\ \overline{37}\ \overline{8}\ \overline{21}\ \overline{25}\ \overline{15}\ \overline{3}$$

Bodily equilibrium

$$\overline{24}\ \overline{16}\ \overline{32}\ \overline{35}\ \overline{1}\ \overline{22}\ \overline{9}$$

Special treats

$$\overline{23}\ \overline{36}\ \overline{7}\ \overline{29}\ \overline{17}\ \overline{26}$$

Broken

$$\overline{11}\ \overline{2}\ \overline{14}\ \overline{19}\ \overline{6}\ \overline{27}\ \overline{39}$$

To dry or shrivel

$$\overline{18}\ \overline{4}\ \overline{31}\ \overline{10}\ \overline{5}\ \overline{13}$$

Not singular

$$\overline{30}\ \overline{12}\ \overline{34}\ \overline{28}\ \overline{20}\ \overline{38}$$

26-9-17-7-3   31-10-5   12-29-28-11   18-4-31-10

23-9-36-17,   35-1-39   13-5-33-29-4-22-27

18-4-31-10   21-17-9-14-24-32-25-1-6.

Day
192

1. AEHJREMI
2. BUEDLO
3. RBNO
4. SHRUENT

5. VEIRDN
6. CUEJSIT
7. EASCSRCAS
8. OARBH

Another son of David who wanted to be king.

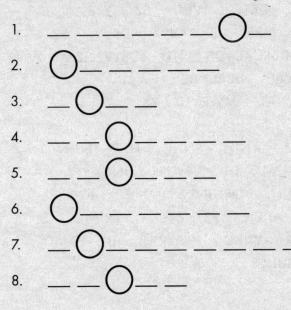

1. __ __ __ __ __ __ ⭕ __
2. ⭕ __ __ __ __ __
3. __ ⭕ __ __
4. __ __ ⭕ __ __ __
5. __ __ ⭕ __ __ __
6. ⭕ __ __ __ __ __
7. __ ⭕ __ __ __ __ __ __ __
8. __ __ ⭕ __ __

Answer: __ __ __ __ __ __ __ __

1. LQTUYV, ZTQ YUPV'G THOV WG OUZ GTUPZQOQV, ZTHZ WZ FHOOUZ GHMQ; OQWZTQP TWG QHP TQHMX, ZTHZ WZ FHOOUZ TQHP.

2. T YTE, DBTQ WUD SZ YTE; VWUFZ MRFF R KVVX DBVV: SZ KTQF DBRUKDVDB JTU DBVV...RA W EUZ WAE DBRUKDZ FWAE, MBVUV AT MWDVU RK.

3. QRUJNRZ ANIFJ JNHC FUR EUJN IQG PRIAJ JH VRYUFR JNGARFY JNRZREUJN: QRUJNRZ ANIFF IQG EHSIQ AJIQV PRYHZR I PRIAJ JH FUR VHEQ JNRZRJH: UJ UA DHQYCAUHQ.

NEW TESTAMENT HEADLINES

1.

MAN BOINDED WHILE TROVELING TO PEROECOTE CHRISTIANS

— — — —

2.

INNOCENO MAN FROED FROM CHAINS AND POISON BY ANSWORED ORAYER

— — — — —

3.

ORIMARY CHRIOTIAO MARTYR SOONOD TO DOATO

— — — — — — —

1 John 5:5

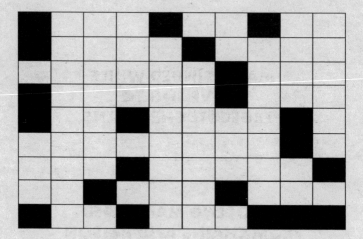

```
C   W   H   T   T   H   T   H   O   N
H   T   M   A   T   D   O   U   E   N
E   O   O   E   L   H   S   V   H   R
I   W   F   E   J   I   D   T   S   E
H   H   E   O   H   O   A   S   H   T
    L   I   R   T   E   S   B   U   T
    A   H   T   V   E   T       T   B
    S   T       G   E
    O
```

PEOPLE OF THE NEW TESTAMENT

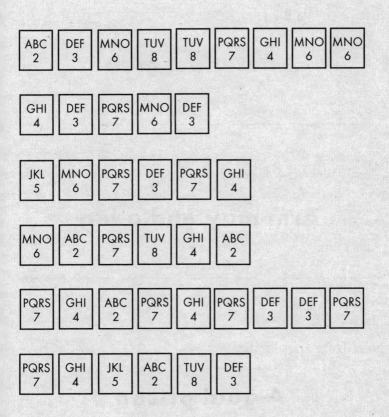

BOOKS OF THE BIBLE. . .

I note last man

— — — — — — — — — — —

WOMEN OF THE BIBLE. . .

Arm may end a leg

— — — —   — — — — — — —

NEW TESTAMENT PEOPLE. . .

A gold prison

— — — — — — — —   — — —

JEREMIAH

EARTHLY	Pumping organ	_____	1.	___ ___
WHERETO	Pitched	_____	2.	___ ___
AFFABLE	Fictional tale	_____	3.	___ ___
SCARLET	Fish skin	_____	4.	___ ___
CHASTEN	Social class	_____	5.	___ ___
NEITHER	Belongs to them	_____	6.	___ ___
DEBORAH	Stuff of life	_____	7.	___ ___
FROSTED	Model T's	_____	8.	___ ___
BRAVEST	Speech parts	_____	9.	___ ___
STEALTH	Smallest	_____	10.	___ ___
HECTARE	Copy	_____	11.	___ ___
WEIGHTS	Vision	_____	12.	___ ___
CHAPMAN	Winner	_____	13.	___ ___

__ __ __ __ __ __ __ __ __ __ __ __ __

__ __ __ __ __ __ __ __ __ __ __ __ __

1 2 3 4 5 6 7 8 9 10 11 12 13

PSALM 7:17

	1	2	3	4	5
1	T	U	G	W	P
2	L	J	Z	D	V
3	E	F	B	M	Q
4	K	H	Y	S	C
5	A	N	I	O	R

53   14-53-21-21   15-55-51-53-44-31   11-42-31

21-54-55-24   51-45-45-54-55-24-53-52-13   11-54

42-53-44   55-53-13-42-11-31-54-12-44-52-31-44-44:

51-52-24   14-53-21-21   44-53-52-13

15-55-51-53-44-31   11-54   11-42-31   52-51-34-31

54-32   11-42-31   21-54-55-24   34-54-44-11

42-53-13-42.

Psalm 3:7

A tiny, brightly colored tropical fish

—— —— —— —— ——
6   23   30   1   14

Easy to love

—— —— —— —— —— —— ——
15   43   38   3   32   21   13

The year of school before first grade

—— —— —— —— —— —— —— —— —— —— —— ——
7   24   33   8   31   41   16   44   35   22   37   26

The study of the stars

—— —— —— —— —— —— —— —— ——
34   12   39   2   29   18   45   4   28

A professional cook

—— —— —— ——
10   17   40   5

To appoint to an office

—— —— —— —— —— —— —— ——
9   42   20   19   11   36   25   27

36-2-24-12-13,   29   15-45-41-8;   12-34-38-27

4-37,   42   4-28   6-43-8:   5-29-35   22-17-42-23

17-44-12-39   12-20-19-39-22-27-11   3-15-21

20-19-9-13   37-26-27-20-24-13-12   23-30-43-33

25-17-40   10-17-13-31-7   32-42-18-13.

Scrambled Circles

1. NMEAIF
2. VOEFGRI
3. AUDHJ
4. ONTNEDC
5. YANIVT
6. KRNOEFAS

7. LFLDEI
8. INTIBHA
9. OAVAINTLS
10. MEERJLUSA
11. SPRTEIS

A well-known sermon was given here.

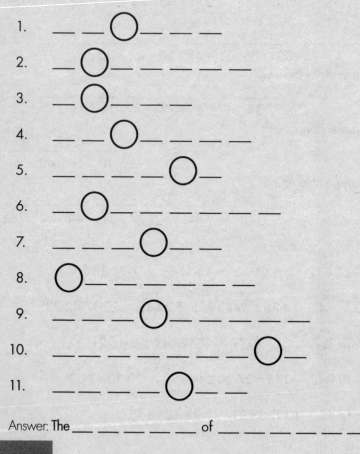

1. __ __ ◯ __ __ __
2. __ ◯ __ __ __ __ __ __
3. __ ◯ __ __ __
4. __ __ ◯ __ __ __
5. __ __ __ __ ◯ __
6. __ ◯ __ __ __ __ __
7. __ __ ◯ __ __
8. ◯ __ __ __ __ __
9. __ __ ◯ __ __ __ __ __
10. __ __ __ __ __ ◯ __
11. __ __ __ ◯ __ __

Answer: The __ __ __ __ __ of __ __ __ __ __ __

1. SGGJ   QGD   TKTHB   XIQ   GQ   CYV
   GAQ   DCYQWV,   UND   TKTHB   XIQ
   ISVG   GQ   DCT   DCYQWV   GM
   GDCTHV.

2. VYC   QAOY   UOBZB   AVC   TPEOC
   QEJA   V   XGZC   FGETO,   AO   BVEC,
   HVJAOP,   EYJG   JAN   AVYCB   E
   TGWWOYC   WN   BSEPEJ: VYC
   AVFEYR   BVEC   JAZB,   AO   RVFO
   ZS   JAO   RAGBJ.

3. IDB   BEB   IDXI   LPFTBID   XI   DYA
   OXIDBQ,   XWR   RBAGYABID   IP
   PJBE   DYA   LPIDBQ,   IDB   QXSBWA
   PO   IDB   SXZZBE   ADXZZ   GYFT   YI
   PNI,   XWR   IDB   EPNWU   BXUZBA
   ADXZZ   BXI   YI.

New Testament Headlines

1.

**PHAROSEE USOS OEANS OF
REOSONINO TO SPORE
APOSTOES' OIVES**

— — — — — — — —

2.

**PERSON BRINGS TO OIGHT
THE DOSTRUCTIVE DIVISIONS
IN A COUROH**

— — — — —

3.

**MON SORVIVES
TERRIBOE SHIPWRECK
AND VIOER BITE**

— — — —

1 JOHN 2:17

O A T D E E D U A E
T R H D R I L F R N
O W O A E A O H T N
D D N H B T T S T B
U T L E W E H E H H
   T O H L H A E S E
   F I E T P O S A W
   H H L   O Y E F G
   D   A   V E T
         R

FOODS IN THE OLD TESTAMENT

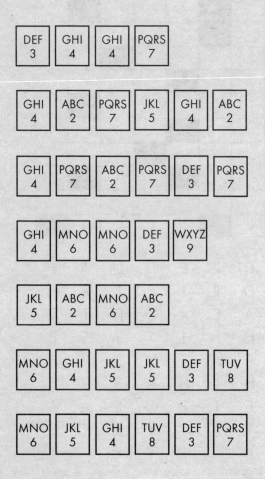

| DEF 3 | GHI 4 | GHI 4 | PQRS 7 |

| GHI 4 | ABC 2 | PQRS 7 | JKL 5 | GHI 4 | ABC 2 |

| GHI 4 | PQRS 7 | ABC 2 | PQRS 7 | DEF 3 | PQRS 7 |

| GHI 4 | MNO 6 | MNO 6 | DEF 3 | WXYZ 9 |

| JKL 5 | ABC 2 | MNO 6 | ABC 2 |

| MNO 6 | GHI 4 | JKL 5 | JKL 5 | DEF 3 | TUV 8 |

| MNO 6 | JKL 5 | GHI 4 | TUV 8 | DEF 3 | PQRS 7 |

BOOKS OF THE BIBLE. . .

He no limp

— — — — — — — —

NEW TESTAMENT PEOPLE. . .

I see harps

— — — — — — — —

WOMEN OF THE BIBLE. . .

O his dare

— — — — — — — —

ROMANS

FRESHEN	Transparent	_____	1. ___ ___
NOTEPAD	Framed glass	_____	2. ___ ___
BREADTH	Restrained	_____	3. ___ ___
GRANITE	Concede	_____	4. ___ ___
LODGING	Leaving	_____	5. ___ ___
FORSAKE	Flatware	_____	6. ___ ___
SHALLOW	Angels' wear	_____	7. ___ ___
INBOARD	Trademark	_____	8. ___ ___
GRAFTED	Graded	_____	9. ___ ___
GUSHING	Utilizing	_____	10. ___ ___
TOPMOST	Walk heavily	_____	11. ___ ___
CITADEL	Sports shoe	_____	12. ___ ___

___ ___ ___ ___ ___ ___ ___ ___ ___ ___ ___ ___ ___

___ ___ ___ ___ ___ ___ ___ ___ ___ ___ ___ ___ ___

1 2 3 4 5 6 7 8 9 10 11 12

Day
208

ECCLESIATES 1:9

	1	2	3	4	5
1	T	U	G	W	P
2	L	J	Z	D	V
3	E	F	B	M	Q
4	K	H	Y	S	C
5	A	N	I	O	R

11-42-31 11-42-53-52-13 11-42-51-11 42-51-11-42

33-31-31-52, 53-44 11-42-51-11 14-42-53-45-42

44-42-51-21-21 33-31; 51-52-24 11-42-51-11

14-42-53-45-42 53-44 24-54-52-31 53-44 11-42-51-11

14-42-53-45-42 44-42-51-21-21 33-31 24-54-52-31:

51-52-24 11-42-31-55-31 53-44 52-54 52-31-14

11-42-53-52-13 12-52-24-31-55 11-42-31 44-12-52.

Acrostic

Psalm 19:14

Land on which crops and/or animals are raised

$\overline{11}$ $\overline{27}$ $\overline{34}$ $\overline{4}$

A perforated pan to drain off liquids

$\overline{13}$ $\overline{39}$ $\overline{36}$ $\overline{5}$ $\overline{26}$ $\overline{12}$ $\overline{41}$ $\overline{21}$

Vacation of a newly married couple

$\overline{6}$ $\overline{43}$ $\overline{15}$ $\overline{42}$ $\overline{22}$ $\overline{10}$ $\overline{28}$ $\overline{16}$ $\overline{3}$

A maze

$\overline{9}$ $\overline{32}$ $\overline{19}$ $\overline{14}$ $\overline{29}$ $\overline{23}$ $\overline{2}$ $\overline{30}$ $\overline{18}$

Motion pictures where parental guidance is suggested

$\overline{40}$ $\overline{44}$ $\overline{31}$ $\overline{1}$ $\overline{45}$ $\overline{38}$ $\overline{24}$ $\overline{37}$

To become too large for

$\overline{7}$ $\overline{25}$ $\overline{17}$ $\overline{33}$ $\overline{20}$ $\overline{35}$ $\overline{8}$

36-42-30   17-18-24   8-7-20-12-37   39-11   10-22

31-28-25-17-18,   32-3-12   17-6-42

10-41-12-23-17-5-17-38-1-26   43-11   31-14

6-24-5-21-17,   19-42   32-13-13-41-40-17-5-19-9-42

38-26   17-18-22   37-38-33-18-17,   16   9-1-29-12,

31-22   37-30-21-42-2-44-17-18,   27-15-12   31-14

29-24-12-42-41-31-24-34.

1. HNSCAEADL

2. NLISA

3. MRUOR

4. CIEVONEL

5. DUMEULTTI

6. EUSMLARJE

These acted as trucks in the ancient times.

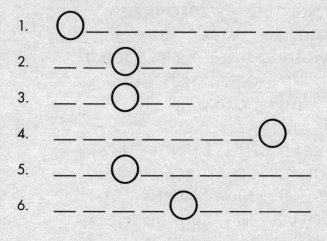

1. ⃝__ __ __ __ __ __ __ __ __

2. __ __ ⃝__ __

3. __ __ ⃝__ __

4. __ __ __ __ __ __ __ ⃝

5. __ __ ⃝__ __ __ __ __

6. __ __ __ __ ⃝__ __ __ __

Answer: __ __ __ __ __ __

CryptoScriptures

1. MTNS AJHV HFS KVPI HFS
   MKVPG IAS AJHV FTZ JQYS:
   WPTJM QJ VDDSPTJM, QJI OVYS
   WSDVPS FTY: BVPZFTE HFS
   KVPI TJ HFS WSQAHG VD
   FVKTJSZZ.

2. UFZ WRZ WUDG ORTRNRF
   QLOZRN UFZ VFZGKOYUFZLFW
   GMPGGZLFW NVPX, UFZ
   TUKWGFGOO RE XGUKY, GDGF
   UO YXG OUFZ YXUY LO RF
   YXG OGU OXRKG.

3. U BCA QPNI HAXNOC BCA
   CAXNB, U BNK BCA NAUSH,
   AGAS BP TUGA AGANK VXS
   XOOPNIUST BP CUH YXKH, XSI
   XOOPNIUST BP BCA ZNLUB PZ
   CUH IPUSTH.

NEW TESTAMENT HEADLINES

1.

**ONLY BEING THAT
COMBINE● ●U●T DI●TY
WITH H●MANITY**

— — — — —

2.

**EV●L QUEEN
●EM●NDS EX●CUTION ●F
●IGOTEOU● BAPTIZER**

— — — — — — —

3.

**D●VOUT MAN
REC●G●IZES BABY AS
THE PRO●I●ED MESS●AH**

E ● N M S I

= Simone

1 Peter 1:16

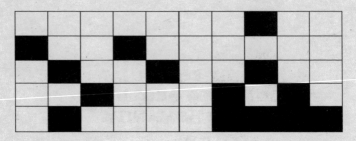

```
L   I   C   E   W   S   E   I   T   E
N   Y   H   F   U   R   I   I   O
M   E   B   A   L   Y   E       H   T
B       S   O   O   R           A
                    Y
```

Apostles

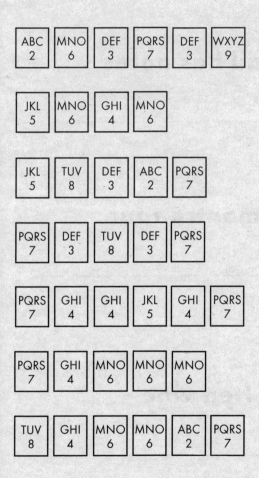

Books of the Bible. . .

Snail has notes

— — — — — — — — — — — —

Places. . .

A mantra tour

— — — — —   — — — — —

Bible Cities. . .

Hen vine

— — — — — — —

Day
216

Ezra

GRAFTED	Wind	_____	1. ___ ___
SIGNORA	Wheat	_____	2. ___ ___
INBOARD	Songbird	_____	3. ___ ___
WEALTHY	Tool	_____	4. ___ ___
HEATHER	Not here	_____	5. ___ ___
FEATHER	Anesthetic	_____	6. ___ ___
BLATANT	Trite	_____	7. ___ ___
ESSENCE	View	_____	8. ___ ___
REBIRTH	Roman river	_____	9. ___ ___
ARBITER	Thorn	_____	10. ___ ___
PLANISH	Aches	_____	11. ___ ___
STENCIL	Pennies	_____	12. ___ ___
WRESTED	Prevent	_____	13. ___ ___

__ __ __ __ __ __ __ __ __ __ __ __ __

__ __ __ __ __ __ __ __ __ __ __ __ __

1 2 3 4 5 6 7 8 9 10 11 12 13

Psalm 20:7

	1	2	3	4	5
1	P	V	Q	C	R
2	W	D	M	S	O
3	G	Z	B	Y	I
4	U	J	F	H	N
5	T	L	E	K	A

24-25-23-53   51-15-41-24-51   35-45

14-44-55-15-35-25-51-24,   55-45-22   24-25-23-53

35-45   44-25-15-24-53-24:   33-41-51   21-53

21-35-52-52   15-53-23-53-23-33-53-15   51-44-53

45-55-23-53   25-43   51-44-53 · 52-25-15-22

25-41-15   31-25-22.

PHILIPPIANS 4:6

The ocean along the west coast of America

$\overline{13}$ $\overline{25}$ $\overline{7}$ $\overline{42}$ $\overline{1}$ $\overline{19}$ $\overline{11}$

A joint in the finger

$\overline{12}$ $\overline{39}$ $\overline{20}$ $\overline{26}$ $\overline{46}$ $\overline{6}$ $\overline{44}$

Excessive, beyond reason

$\overline{18}$ $\overline{10}$ $\overline{45}$ $\overline{29}$ $\overline{49}$ $\overline{24}$ $\overline{47}$ $\overline{5}$ $\overline{40}$ $\overline{17}$ $\overline{34}$

Evoking a question

$\overline{9}$ $\overline{33}$ $\overline{2}$ $\overline{43}$ $\overline{21}$ $\overline{35}$ $\overline{51}$ $\overline{14}$ $\overline{31}$ $\overline{3}$ $\overline{52}$ $\overline{48}$

Articles such as tools, utensils, and nails

$\overline{36}$ $\overline{38}$ $\overline{15}$ $\overline{27}$ $\overline{22}$ $\overline{55}$ $\overline{4}$ $\overline{54}$

A person sent to a foreign country for ministry

$\overline{30}$ $\overline{8}$ $\overline{53}$ $\overline{37}$ $\overline{32}$ $\overline{50}$ $\overline{16}$ $\overline{28}$ $\overline{41}$ $\overline{23}$

3-44   11-40-4-2-1-20-6   1-50-15

16-50-21-36-32-14-5;   3-20-21   42-17

18-24-44-29-23   34-36-8-17-5   3-23   13-29-38-23-48-41

49-39-27   53-33-13-13-6-19-26-25-21-35-51-16

22-8-21-36   21-36-28-16-46-37-5-32-24-35-16-5

52-18-34   23-51-20-29   15-44-9-20-2-37-45-43   3-48

30-31-27-54   12-39-50-22-16   33-14-21-51   5-50-27.

Scrambled Circles

1. ISEMT
2. NOURD
3. DUNRE
4. NINOISTCURT
5. CHKTI

6. HSTIG
7. MOCEUNS
8. ARSOVI
9. NERTAMN
10. UERBEK

Another name for Mount Sinai.

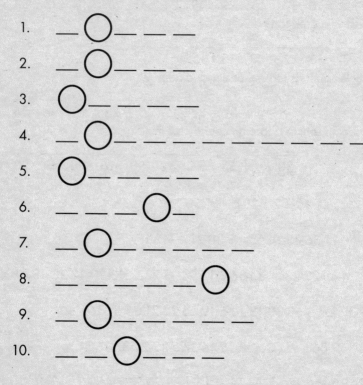

1. _ ◯ _ _ _
2. _ ◯ _ _ _
3. ◯ _ _ _ _
4. _ ◯ _ _ _ _ _ _ _ _ _
5. ◯ _ _ _ _
6. _ _ _ ◯ _
7. _ ◯ _ _ _ _ _
8. _ _ _ _ _ ◯
9. _ ◯ _ _ _ _ _
10. _ _ ◯ _ _ _

Answer: _ _ _ _ _ _   _ _ _ _ _ _

1. JIT JIOTC PFRTJI XFJ, KWJ CFG
   JF ZJTSV, SXH JF DOVV, SXH JF
   HTZJGFA: O SR PFRT JISJ JITA
   ROYIJ ISBT VOCT, SXH JISJ JITA
   ROYIJ ISBT OJ RFGT
   SKWXHSXJVA.

2. WHN BSM STXGQRE KX BSM
   SMQE HW BSM ZKWM, MLMR
   QX OSNKXB KX BSM SMQE HW
   BSM OSTNOS: QRE SM KX BSM
   XQLKHTN HW BSM GHEV.

3. CKW SII XNSX OD OJ XNB
   PKWIA, XNB IEDX KC XNB
   CIBDN, SJA XNB IEDX KC XNB
   BRBD, SJA XNB LWOAB KC IOCB,
   OD JKX KC XNB CSXNBW, TEX
   OD KC XNB PKWIA.

Spotty Headlines

New Testament Headlines

1.

**RESPEC●ABLE ●ER●ON
●AP●IZED ●IS COUSI●
IN ●●E ●ORD●N ROV●R**

— — — —   — — —

— — — — — — —

2.

**WRITING ●ETTERS
CONTIN●ES BY
UND●UNTED ●RISONER**

— — — —

3.

**DOUB●ING FI●H●●●AN
●ULLS IN ●NOUGH F●SH
TO SI●K B●AT**

— — — — —   — — — —

Day
222

Bible Quotation

1 Samuel 12:22

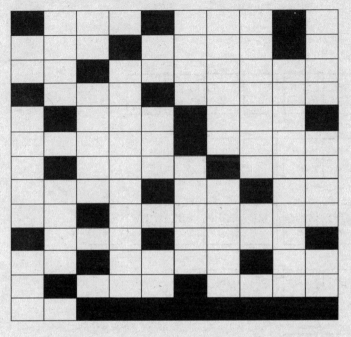

```
E   F   I   F   W   T   H   L   K   L
G   R   F   S   O   I   L   A   P   N
S   T   E   O   A   R   S   O   S   E
T   T   H   A   S   P   E   I   M   O
U   O   S   A   T   E   A   A   E   P
L   E   S   E   K   L   O   E   H   C
O   U   H   M   R   K   E   E   E   A
O   H   O   I   L   E   H   B   D   L
A   H   D   R   E   H   S   R   Y   D
T   R   E   P   I   N   P   R   O   E
        P           T
```

GIANTS

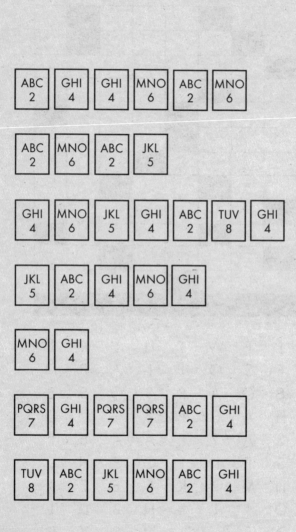

BOOKS OF THE BIBLE. . .

I jam here

— — — — — — — —

KINGS. . .

Rob a home

— — — — — — —

NEW TESTAMENT PEOPLE. . .

Mice sound

— — — — — — — — —

Drop Two

JOB

OCTOPUS	To lower oneself	_____	1. __ __
COLONEL	Violinlike instrument	_____	2. __ __
MANTELS	Slants	_____	3. __ __
STARDOM	Small missiles	_____	4. __ __
GUILDER	Reigned	_____	5. __ __
DETROIT	Attempted	_____	6. __ __
DAMPING	Mimicking	_____	7. __ __
WORLDLY	Humorous	_____	8. __ __
CLAMOUR	Wall art	_____	9. __ __
UNAIDED	Ate	_____	10. __ __
UNCLOSE	Ice cream holders	_____	11. __ __
SCALDED	Image for transfer	_____	12. __ __
MILEAGE	Small light	_____	13. __ __

__ __ __ __ __ __ __ __ __ __ __ __ __

__ __ __ __ __ __ __ __ __ __ __ __ __

1　2　3　4　5　6　7　8　9　10　11　12　13

Day 226

Philippians 4:13

	1	2	3	4	5
1	P	V	Q	C	R
2	W	D	M	S	O
3	G	Z	B	Y	I
4	U	J	F	H	N
5	T	L	E	K	A

35   14-55-45   22-25   55-52-52   51-44-35-45-31-24

51-44-15-25-41-31-44   14-44-15-35-24-51

21-44-35-14-44   24-51-15-53-45-31-51-44-53-45-53-51-44

23-53.

PHILIPPIANS 2:3

Any day except Saturday and Sunday

—— —— —— —— —— —— ——
29 14 1 6 27 41 37

To steal money from an employer

—— —— —— —— —— —— —— ——
20 36 13 44 5 28 22 12

Flawless

—— —— —— —— —— —— ——
15 38 30 19 43 31 4

The area in which a baseball team waits between innings

—— —— —— —— —— ——
16 34 7 23 3 21

To dissolve into the air

—— —— —— —— —— —— —— —— ——
24 8 33 2 32 17 40 11 26

The current style of dress

—— —— —— —— —— —— ——
10 35 25 18 42 39 9

22-20-4   9-39-11-18-42-9-7   13-44   16-39-9-26

11-18-17-39-3-7-18   25-4-30-42-19-38   23-30

8-41-42-9-7-22-39-30-37;   13-34-4   42-9

22-23-29-22-42-9-43-25-25   32-10   36-42-9-27

22-38-4   24-33-31-18   38-25-4-20-14-36

32-4-18-43-30   13-1-4-21-43-30   11-18-35-9

21-18-43-36-25-1-22-8-24-25.

1. EELZIEK
2. DKMOIGN
3. IEATPHOI
4. CELARCNBU
5. HPOHAAR
6. ELDITF

7. ILASN
8. BETLERIR
9. DEJGU
10. APECHROR
11. HHNEAET

These two men went to heaven without dying.

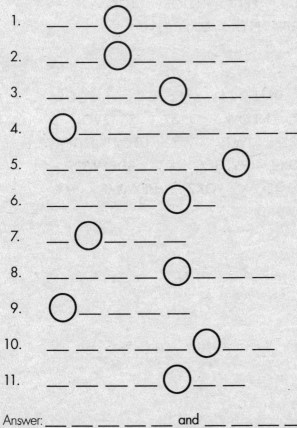

1. __ __ ◯ __ __ __ __
2. __ __ ◯ __ __ __
3. __ __ __ __ ◯ __ __ __
4. ◯ __ __ __ __ __ __ __ __
5. __ __ __ __ __ __ ◯
6. __ __ __ __ ◯ __
7. __ ◯ __ __ __ __
8. __ __ __ ◯ __ __ __
9. ◯ __ __ __ __
10. __ __ __ __ __ ◯ __ __
11. __ __ __ __ ◯ __ __

Answer: __ __ __ __ __ **and** __ __ __ __ __ __ __

Day 229

1. ZO   QPGDD,   YXR   EXWI   PLYP   G
   YC   MWR: G   IGDD   ZO   OHYDPOR
   YCWXM   PLO   LOYPLOX,   G   IGDD
   ZO   OHYDPOR   GX   PLO   OYTPL.

2. LO   PLYP   GQ   QDWI   PW   YXMOT
   GQ   ZOPPOT   PLYX   PLO   CGMLPB;
   YXR   LO   PLYP   TFDOPL   LGQ
   QNGTGP   PLYX   LO   PLYP
   PYEOPL   Y   JGPB.

3. IZPNP   DEPLZTZA,   MZTJGR,   MZTJGR,
   J   PDR   NEOW   OKZZ,   ZSBZVO   D
   FDE   CZ   CWTE   WY   LDOZT   DEA
   WY   OKZ   PVJTJO,   KZ   BDEEWO
   ZEOZT   JEOW   OKZ   HJEXAWF   WY
   XWA.

New Testament Headlines

1.

**●OUNG ●AN
S●RUGGLES TO PAS●OR
FLEDGL●NG C●URCH**

— — — — — — —

2.

**R●NAWAY ●LAV● BEC●●ES
A CHRI●T●A●**

— — — — — — — —

3.

**●ONGU● OF FI●E
SAT U●ON SUDD●NLY
MULTILINGUAL MAN**

— — — — —

PHILIPPIANS 1:6

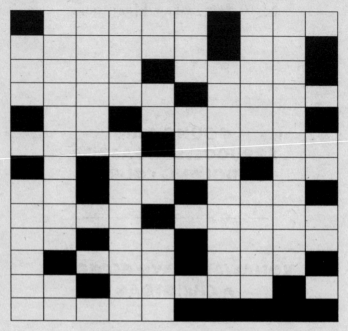

F	I	D	I	N	S	T	N	O	N
T	H	I	L	N	H	I	A	F	C
R	H	I	I	T	B	E	S	Y	T
L	H	T	J	E	P	D	R	A	O
O	A	E	S	E	G	Y	H	H	I
H	A	I	I	G	T	E	C	U	N
R	F	L	E	W	V	E	O	W	O
H	R	E	S	O	O	D	R	U	
T	B	T	H	N		U	C	F	
W	I		N	T		U	O	T	
	M		H				G	Y	
	K		G						

Telephone Scrambles

MUSICAL INSTRUMENTS

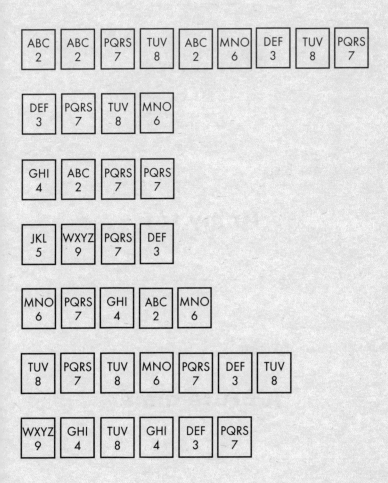

Events. . .

Not a rice

— — — — — — —

Books of the Bible. . .

Hi my tot

— — — — — — —

New Testament People. . .

A brute aims

— — — — — — — — —

Ruth

SCARLET	Loves	_____	1. __ __
NIGHTLY	Knotting	_____	2. __ __
BLARNEY	Discover	_____	3. __ __
PLEASES	Gross receipts	_____	4. __ __
INFLAME	Last	_____	5. __ __
ALIMONY	Italian city	_____	6. __ __
PROPHET	Spasm	_____	7. __ __
MISDEAL	Female servants	_____	8. __ __
COASTER	Vehicles	_____	9. __ __
SPARING	Corn	_____	10. __ __
SHINGLE	Burn	_____	11. __ __
EATABLE	Sheep sound	_____	12. __ __

__ __ __ __ __ __ __ __ __ __ __ __

__ __ __ __ __ __ __ __ __ __ __ __

1 2 3 4 5 6 7 8 9 10 11 12

Matthew 5:44

	1	2	3	4	5
1	P	V	Q	C	R
2	W	D	M	S	O
3	G	Z	B	Y	I
4	U	J	F	H	N
5	T	L	E	K	A

52-25-12-53   34-25-41-15   53-45-53-23-35-53-24,

33-52-53-24-24   51-44-53-23   51-44-55-51

14-41-15-24-53   34-25-41,   22-25   31-25-25-22

51-25   51-44-53-23   51-44-55-51   44-55-51-53   34-25-41,

55-45-22   11-15-55-34   43-25-15   51-44-53-23

21-44-35-14-44   22-53-24-11-35-51-53-43-41-52-52-34

41-24-53   34-25-41,   55-45-22

11-53-15-24-53-14-41-51-53   34-25-41.

PSALM 19:1

A large tank used for storing liquids

$\overline{}$ $\overline{}$ $\overline{}$
11   36   12

The arrangement of a dance

$\overline{}$ $\overline{}$ $\overline{}$ $\overline{}$ $\overline{}$ $\overline{}$ $\overline{}$ $\overline{}$ $\overline{}$ $\overline{}$ $\overline{}$ $\overline{}$
7   35   19   42   27   39   1   43   20   45   28   8

Lack of hope

$\overline{}$ $\overline{}$ $\overline{}$ $\overline{}$ $\overline{}$ $\overline{}$ $\overline{}$
2   38   9   34   26   17   21

Laboring

$\overline{}$ $\overline{}$ $\overline{}$ $\overline{}$ $\overline{}$ $\overline{}$ $\overline{}$
18   41   25   33   10   6   16

Erroneous thinking

$\overline{}$ $\overline{}$ $\overline{}$ $\overline{}$ $\overline{}$ $\overline{}$ $\overline{}$ $\overline{}$ $\overline{}$
4   22   40   13   3   37   29   23   15

The art of folding paper

$\overline{}$ $\overline{}$ $\overline{}$ $\overline{}$ $\overline{}$ $\overline{}$ $\overline{}$
14   32   31   44   24   30   5

12-35-27   35-23-36-11-23-6-9   2-3-7-37-20-32-3

12-28-27   44-37-19-21-8   14-15   1-39-2;

20-6-2   12-35-3   15-5-21-4-24-30-23-6-12

40-35-27-18-38-12-28   35-22-9

28-26-6-2-8-18-41-25-33.

Scrambled Circles

1. NRUGBIN
2. OENSSA
3. TMTARE
4. AODHTNUS
5. NPESARIS
6. NSITEG
7. AYREL

This town was known as Jesus' home away from home.

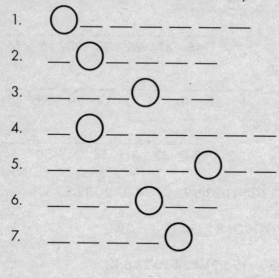

1. ⭕ __ __ __ __ __ __
2. __ ⭕ __ __ __ __
3. __ __ __ ⭕ __ __
4. __ ⭕ __ __ __ __ __ __
5. __ __ __ __ __ ⭕ __ __
6. __ __ __ ⭕ __ __
7. __ __ __ __ ⭕

Answer: __ __ __ __ __ __ __

1. SJPAAPQ   LA   BMP   ITU   BMTB
   PUQCYPBM   BPIWBTBLVU: OVY
   EMPU   MP   LA   BYLPQ,   MP   AMTJJ
   YPRPLDP   BMP   RYVEU   VO   JLOP,
   EMLRM   BMP   JVYQ   MTBM
   WYVILAPQ   BV   BMPI   BMTB   JVDP
   MLI.

2. GXY   XEYD   TDX   YMFY   KJFA   RT
   EFRJ   ZMFQQ   YMJ   ZXE   DK
   ANLMYJDXZEJZZ   FANZJ   VNYM
   MJFQNEL   NE   MNZ   VNELZ;   FEI
   TJ   ZMFQQ   LD   KDAYM,   FEI   LADV
   XC   FZ   BFQWJZ   DK   YMJ   ZYFQQ.

3. MDL   UDP   XCTB   TDB   RFX   XDT
   FTBD   BRC   ZDLHP   BD   WDTPCVT
   BRC   ZDLHP;   EIB   BRQB   BRC
   ZDLHP   BRLEDIR   RFV   VFURB   EC
   XQNCP.

New Testament Headlines

1.

**CHRISTI●● ●ELIEVED TO ●E
ORDE●ED TO ●CCOMP●NY
EX-PERSECUTOR OF CHRI●TIANS**

— — — — — — — — — —

2.

**●ULER SLAUG●TERE● ALL
MALE BABIES IN H●PE OF
●LIMINATING FUTURE KING**

— — — — — — —

3.

**●BSENT ●AN D●UB●S
RE●URRECTION T●EORY**

— — — — — — —

Psalm 18:32

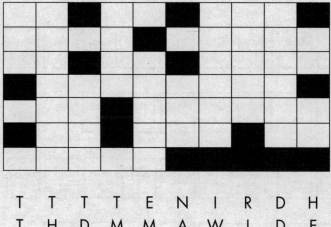

T	T	T	T	E	N	I	R	D	H
T	H	D	M	M	A	W	I	D	E
A	H	Y	C	S	G	G	E	T	E
I	S	A	I	W	A	Y	O	P	H
R	N	E	R	T	G	T	T	H	
	M		E	E	K		H		
	F								

Telephone Scrambles

CITIES IN THE NEW TESTAMENT

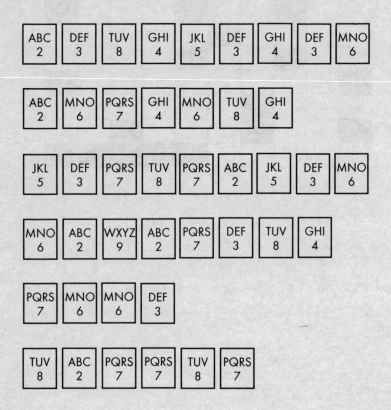

| ABC 2 | DEF 3 | TUV 8 | GHI 4 | JKL 5 | DEF 3 | GHI 4 | DEF 3 | MNO 6 |

| ABC 2 | MNO 6 | PQRS 7 | GHI 4 | MNO 6 | TUV 8 | GHI 4 |

| JKL 5 | DEF 3 | PQRS 7 | TUV 8 | PQRS 7 | ABC 2 | JKL 5 | DEF 3 | MNO 6 |

| MNO 6 | ABC 2 | WXYZ 9 | ABC 2 | PQRS 7 | DEF 3 | TUV 8 | GHI 4 |

| PQRS 7 | MNO 6 | MNO 6 | DEF 3 |

| TUV 8 | ABC 2 | PQRS 7 | PQRS 7 | TUV 8 | PQRS 7 |

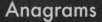

BOOKS OF THE BIBLE. . .

Snag a tail

— — — — — — — — —

NEW TESTAMENT PEOPLE. . .

A moot grains ad

— — — —

— — — — — — — —

RIVERS/BODIES OF WATER. . .

Reed meant rain

— — — — — — — — — — — — — —

Galatians

BEATLES	Rent	_____	1. ___ ___
HECKLER	Salesperson	_____	2. ___ ___
ANTIQUE	One of five	_____	3. ___ ___
REDRESS	Plant starters	_____	4. ___ ___
STYGIAN	Goliath	_____	5. ___ ___
BEDSIDE	Agreed with	_____	6. ___ ___
ONEROUS	Sleep noise	_____	7. ___ ___
REGNANT	Representative	_____	8. ___ ___
SWARMED	Heats	_____	9. ___ ___
ANOTHER	Brier	_____	10. ___ ___
NOCTURN	Woo	_____	11. ___ ___
ONWARDS	Sketched	_____	12. ___ ___

___ ___ ___ ___ ___ ___ ___ ___ ___ ___ ___ ___

___ ___ ___ ___ ___ ___ ___ ___ ___ ___ ___ ___

1   2   3   4   5   6   7   8   9   10   11   12

Day 244

Proverbs 30:5

	1	2	3	4	5
1	P	V	Q	C	R
2	W	D	M	S	O
3	G	Z	B	Y	I
4	U	J	F	H	N
5	T	L	E	K	A

53-12-53-15-34   21-25-15-22   25-43   31-25-22

35-24   11-41-15-53:   44-53   35-24   55

24-44-35-53-52-22   41-45-51-25   51-44-53-23

51-44-55-51   11-41-51   51-44-53-35-15

51-15-41-24-51   35-45   44-35-23.

ROMANS 12:9

An opening in a building for letting in light or air

___ ___ ___ ___ ___ ___
16 22   5 28 32 20

An understanding after an event of what should have been done

___ ___ ___ ___ ___ ___ ___ ___ ___
14 36   6 21   1 42 37 26   9

Usable

___ ___ ___ ___ ___ ___
 3 15 41   8 27 33

The month after February

___ ___ ___ ___ ___
19 39 13 10 31

Innocent

___ ___ ___ ___ ___ ___ ___ ___ ___
38 11 35 23 43 17 25   4 30

Migraine

___ ___ ___ ___ ___ ___ ___ ___
 2 34   7 24 29 18 12 40

27-33-9   23-32-3-25   8-40   16-35-9-31-32-11-43

21-15-1-30-15-19-11-27-7-9-22-32-5.   39-8-14-32-13

43-2-7-43   20-12-35-18-31   36-1   25-3-42-17;

10-27-34-41-3-25   43-32   43-2-29-43

16-26-22-18-2   42-4   37-32-32-24.

Scrambled Circles

1. WDEPOL
2. TEHELB
3. DVDIDEI
4. SCNEINE
5. GMIEAS
6. RENTUR
7. HRBESACN
8. RPDAET
9. NDEOIRIS

The great devourer as described in Job.

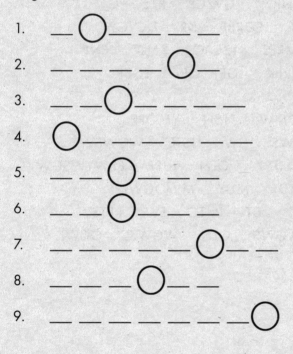

1. __ ⃝ __ __ __ __
2. __ __ __ __ ⃝ __
3. __ __ ⃝ __ __ __ __
4. ⃝ __ __ __ __ __
5. __ __ ⃝ __ __ __
6. __ __ ⃝ __ __ __
7. __ __ __ __ __ ⃝ __ __
8. __ __ __ ⃝ __ __
9. __ __ __ __ __ __ ⃝

Answer: __ __ __ __ __ __ __ __ __ __

1. CDAN ZDRHC MAC CRXB CDB
   MRUB AJ CDB HAVQ CDT WAQ
   OM EROM; JAV CDB HAVQ YOHH
   MAC DAHQ DOU WNOHCHBZZ
   CDRC CRXBCD DOZ MRUB OM EROM.

2. GRF ENPVP GVZCP RZE G
   AVZANPE CDRBP DR DCVGPI
   IDXP MREZ TZCPC, KNZT ENP
   IZVF XRPK LGBP EZ LGBP.

3. OLN DMW PTSN YMOPP
   NWPUGWS CW HSTC WGWSV
   WGUP ITSX, OLN IUPP ESWYWSGW
   CW ZLDT MUY MWOGWLPV
   XULRNTC: DT IMTC FW RPTSV
   HTS WGWS OLN WGWS. OCWL.

NEW TESTAMENT HEADLINES

1.

**MAN DEAD FO● FO●R D●YS
COME● B●CK TO ●IFE
WITH ●EST**

— — — — — — —

2.

**●URIOUS PHAROS●E SEEKS
TO●GH AN●WERS IN
●ID●LE OF ●IGHT**

— — — — — — — —

3.

**F●ITHFUL MAN
●ENERO●SLY HELP●
FELLOW BEL●EVERS**

— — — — —

Jeremiah 29:13

```
T   L   N   D   S   Y   H   K   S   D
A   Y   L   H   D   E   E   I   A   Y
E   M   A   I   T   F   E   N   N   E
E   E   E   N   R   H   N   A   L   M
A   A   S   U   A   H   F   L   S   H
E   R   C   H   W   L   L   E   S   M
        W       E       O       R   H
        O               E           L
                                    R
```

CONVERSIONS IN THE NEW TESTAMENT

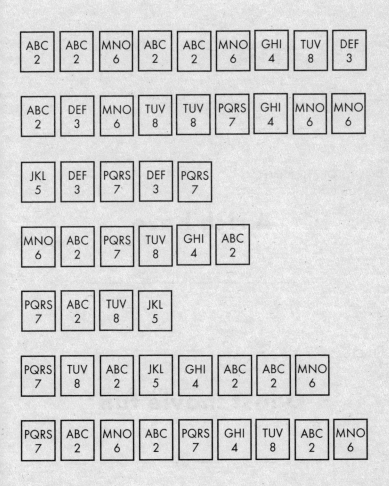

| ABC 2 | ABC 2 | MNO 6 | ABC 2 | ABC 2 | MNO 6 | GHI 4 | TUV 8 | DEF 3 |

| ABC 2 | DEF 3 | MNO 6 | TUV 8 | TUV 8 | PQRS 7 | GHI 4 | MNO 6 | MNO 6 |

| JKL 5 | DEF 3 | PQRS 7 | DEF 3 | PQRS 7 |

| MNO 6 | ABC 2 | PQRS 7 | TUV 8 | GHI 4 | ABC 2 |

| PQRS 7 | ABC 2 | TUV 8 | JKL 5 |

| PQRS 7 | TUV 8 | ABC 2 | JKL 5 | GHI 4 | ABC 2 | ABC 2 | MNO 6 |

| PQRS 7 | ABC 2 | MNO 6 | ABC 2 | PQRS 7 | GHI 4 | TUV 8 | ABC 2 | MNO 6 |

BAD GUYS. . .

I joust as I card

_ _ _ _ _

_ _ _ _ _ _ _ _

BOOKS OF THE BIBLE. . .

A rich haze

_ _ _ _ _ _ _ _ _

PLACES. . .

O lost movie fun

_ _ _ _ _ _ _

_ _ _ _ _ _

JOHN

CORONET	Sing	_____	1. ___ ___
HABITED	Decreased	_____	2. ___ ___
ANDIRON	Deplete	_____	3. ___ ___
CAPTURE	Prank	_____	4. ___ ___
HOMERIC	Felony	_____	5. ___ ___
BEATING	Human	_____	6. ___ ___
SLAVISH	Closed vessels	_____	7. ___ ___
TENSILE	Clothes ropes	_____	8. ___ ___
SWARMED	Imagine	_____	9. ___ ___
COASTER	Grocery helps	_____	10. ___ ___
REDSKIN	Glided over snow	_____	11. ___ ___
LAMBERT	Dark yellow	_____	12. ___ ___
MILDEST	Set of steps	_____	13. ___ ___

__ __ __ __ __ __ __ __ __ __ __ __ __

__ __ __ __ __ __ __ __ __ __ __ __ __

1 2 3 4 5 6 7 8 9 10 11 12 13

Day 253

JAMES 1:5

	1	2	3	4	5
1	P	V	Q	C	R
2	W	D	M	S	O
3	G	Z	B	Y	I
4	U	J	F	H	N
5	T	L	E	K	A

35-43   55-45-34   25-43   34-25-41   52-55-14-54

21-35-24-22-25-23,   52-53-51   44-35-23   55-24-54

25-43   31-25-22,   51-44-55-51   31-35-12-53-51-44

51-25   55-52-52   23-53-45   52-35-33-53-15-55-52-52-34,

55-45-22   41-11-33-15-55-35-22-53-51-44   45-25-51;

55-45-22   35-51   24-44-55-52-52   33-53

31-35-12-53-45   44-35-23.

ROMANS 12:21

Getting back at someone

$\overline{20}$ $\overline{29}$ $\overline{5}$ $\overline{16}$ $\overline{11}$ $\overline{2}$ $\overline{22}$

A piece of furniture to sit on

$\overline{4}$ $\overline{18}$ $\overline{7}$ $\overline{10}$ $\overline{32}$

To remove an arm or leg, usually in surgery

$\overline{28}$ $\overline{12}$ $\overline{35}$ $\overline{17}$ $\overline{25}$ $\overline{3}$ $\overline{21}$ $\overline{34}$

Made from a tree

$\overline{15}$ $\overline{23}$ $\overline{19}$ $\overline{1}$ $\overline{26}$ $\overline{8}$

Costing nothing

$\overline{13}$ $\overline{31}$ $\overline{9}$ $\overline{24}$

To assess fault

$\overline{27}$ $\overline{33}$ $\overline{6}$ $\overline{14}$ $\overline{30}$

27-34   11-19-25   23-5-29-20-4-23-12-16   19-13

26-5-10-33,   27-17-25   23-5-22-31-4-19-14-30

9-5-10-33   15-10-21-18   2-23-19-1.

Scrambled Circles

1. NUTJDEMG
2. CHEKOML
3. NREGVA
4. URSUPE
5. ESIFIMHC

6. OFWLAL
7. LTUTUM
8. RAEDEP
9. RMERDU

King David established this city as the capital of Israel and Judah.

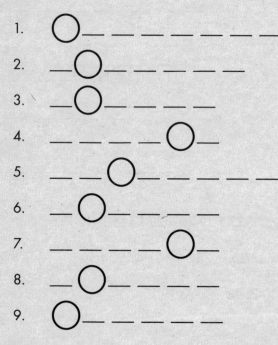

1. ◯ __ __ __ __ __ __ __ __
2. __ ◯ __ __ __ __ __ __
3. __ ◯ __ __ __ __ __
4. __ __ __ __ ◯ __
5. __ __ ◯ __ __ __ __ __
6. __ ◯ __ __ __ __
7. __ __ __ __ ◯ __
8. __ ◯ __ __ __ __
9. ◯ __ __ __ __

Answer: __ __ __ __ __ __ __ __ __

1. YS BOAI DATNGYA BOSG NHB
   UGZAENHR, NIJ IAWBOAH TSUJ
   ISH OSB, W EWUU YXGA BOAA
   SGB SQ RL RSGBO.

2. KTI TWY YVZ FKXXLUQF FVWN?
   KXLQU, KTI EU EKDFLMUI, KTI
   YKQV KYKZ FVZ QLTQ, PKGGLTO
   WT FVU TKSU WC FVU GWXI.

3. IZ NSRWW BCWCJZXYWI VZZF
   YSZ OQEERXBEZXYN QG YSZ
   WQAB IQHA JQB, RXB SCN
   YZNYCEQXCZN, RXB SCN
   NYRYHYZN, DSCOS SZ SRYS
   OQEERXBZB YSZZ.

NEW TESTAMENT HEADLINES

1.

BRAVE MAN ATTEMPTS TO WALK ON WATER

— — — — —

2.

OVER FIVE THOUSAND PEOPLE ARE FED BY ONE MAN

— — — — —

3.

ARROGANT DOMINEERING MAN REJECTS APOSTOLIC AUTHORITY

— — — — — — — — — — —

PSALM 73:28

```
M  B  E  T  M  I  O  O  R  L
S  G  C  O  N  R  M  R  A  K
L  E  U  T  A  H  E  O  Y  W
H  N  O  T  H  Y  D  O  A  G
D  D  R  L  Y  G  T  T  E  S
L  U  T  H  D  O  A  H  R  U
S  T  T  I  O  R  W  V  R  T
O  O  T  I  R  I  T  A  I  T
P  A  E  D  I     F  D  E
   E        A        T
```

Day
259

Telephone Scrambles

Names for Christ

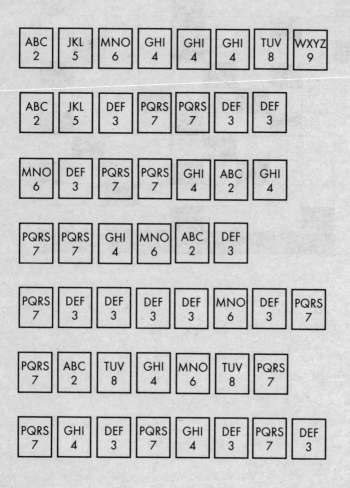

Day 260

BIBLE CITIES. . .

A sud scam

_ _ _ _ _ _ _ _

BOOKS OF THE BIBLE. . .

Undo mere toy

_ _ _ _ _ _ _ _ _ _

PLACES. . .

Atom is a poem

_ _ _ _ _ _ _ _ _ _ _

Day 261

TITUS

CHEETAH	Instruct	_____	1. __ __
FLOATER	Another time	_____	2. __ __
LEATHER	Not here	_____	3. __ __
DIEHARD	Listened	_____	4. __ __
DIALECT	Woven	_____	5. __ __
HARMONY	City official	_____	6. __ __
FREIGHT	Not our	_____	7. __ __
FEARFUL	Beacon	_____	8. __ __
CAPITOL	Theme	_____	9. __ __
SWARMED	Fantasize	_____	10. __ __
ENDMOST	Darns	_____	11. __ __
STEWART	Refuse	_____	12. __ __
DOLTISH	Works	_____	13. __ __

— — — — — — — — — — — — —

— — — — — — — — — — — — —

1 2 3 4 5 6 7 8 9 10 11 12 13

Day
262

Psalm 5:8

	1	2	3	4	5
1	P	V	Q	C	R
2	W	D	M	S	O
3	G	Z	B	Y	I
4	U	J	F	H	N
5	T	L	E	K	A

52-53-55-22   23-53,   25   52-25-15-22,   35-45

51-44-34   15-35-31-44-51-53-25-41-24-45-53-24-24

33-53-14-55-41-24-53   25-43   23-35-45-53

53-45-53-23-35-53-24;   23-55-54-53   51-44-34

21-55-34   24-51-15-55-35-31-44-51

33-53-43-25-15-53   23-34   43-55-14-53.

1 CORINTHIANS 10:31

To make someone laugh by a touch

$\overline{10}$ $\overline{36}$ $\overline{32}$ $\overline{3}$ $\overline{26}$ $\overline{43}$

A creature said to have breathed fire

$\overline{39}$ $\overline{9}$ $\overline{30}$ $\overline{14}$ $\overline{19}$ $\overline{2}$

Foolishness

$\overline{31}$ $\overline{11}$ $\overline{15}$ $\overline{6}$ $\overline{23}$

A forked breastbone in most birds

$\overline{16}$ $\overline{42}$ $\overline{24}$ $\overline{1}$ $\overline{12}$ $\overline{28}$ $\overline{4}$ $\overline{33}$

The science of farming

$\overline{35}$ $\overline{5}$ $\overline{25}$ $\overline{45}$ $\overline{40}$ $\overline{27}$ $\overline{22}$ $\overline{13}$ $\overline{38}$ $\overline{29}$ $\overline{20}$

Able to shield from injury

$\overline{18}$ $\overline{8}$ $\overline{41}$ $\overline{34}$ $\overline{21}$ $\overline{7}$ $\overline{37}$ $\overline{46}$ $\overline{17}$ $\overline{44}$

16-1-43-13-1-21-29   37-1-33-25-43-31-41-29-33

23-21   20-35-10,   19-8   39-25-36-2-3,   11-8

16-1-30-13-24-41-44-17-21-9   23-20   39-28,   39-19

35-22-15   13-41   34-1-43   14-26-28-25-23

41-31   5-28-39.

Scrambled Circles

1. AOHBIAD
2. ETLSUBB
3. YIMTHG
4. IRNEMA

5. DISFLE
6. STHTRI
7. LPRIAEV
8. ERBSEHCA

She was the mother of Ahaziah.

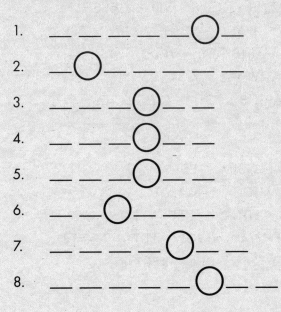

1. __ __ __ __ __ ◯ __

2. __ ◯ __ __ __ __ __

3. __ __ __ ◯ __ __

4. __ __ __ ◯ __ __

5. __ __ __ ◯ __ __

6. __ ◯ __ __ __

7. __ __ __ __ ◯ __ __

8. __ __ __ __ __ ◯ __ __

Answer: __ __ __ __ __ __ __ __

1. ERPQ   YILB   XSI   PEBC,   LRC
   KIBMI   SVF   VR   XBHXS   TVXS   LPP
   QEHB   SILBX: YEB   OERKVCIB   SET
   DBILX   XSVRDK   SI   SLXS   CERI
   YEB   QEH.

2. TYDYKVPYZYBB   CSK   VPI   UKYGV
   QYKALYB'   BGEY   VPSH   JLJBV   TSV
   HVVYKZI   ASTBHQY   VPYQ,   TSK
   CSKBGEY   VPYQ;   CSK   VPSH   GKV
   G   UKGALSHB   GTJ   QYKALCHZ
   USJ.

3. FSB   MT   GSIM   EDFE   FYY
   EDLSQZ   MICG   EIQTEDTC   JIC
   QIIB   EI   EDTN   EDFE   YIAT   QIB,
   EI   EDTN   MDI   FCT   EDT   VFYYTB
   FVVICBLSQ   EI   DLZ   KPCKIZT.

NEW TESTAMENT HEADLINES

1.

**ONLᐧ VIRGIN WOᐧAN
EVER TO GIVE BIᐧTH
TO BᐧBY SON**

— — — —

2.

**ᐧᐧEATLY DEᐧON-POSSᐧSSED
WOᐧAᐧ IS FINᐧLLᐧ HᐧALED
ᐧND CᐧEᐧNSEᐧ**

— — — —

— — — — — — — —

3.

**ᐧAREFUL MOTHᐧR
UNKNOWINGLY PRᐧPARES SOᐧ
FOR FᐧTURE MINᐧSTRY**

— — — — — —

COLOSSIANS 3:2

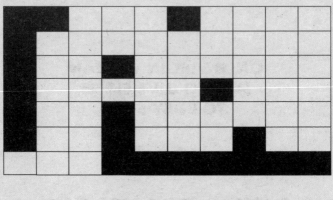

```
R  O  S  O  E  C  I  N  U  N
   A  F  E  T  H  E  N  O  S
   O  N  F  V  E  T  O  G  A
   A  N     T  H  Y  I  E  R
   O  H     T  H  I  N  G  T
   T  B     T        O  S
      N
```

CITIES IN THE OLD TESTAMENT

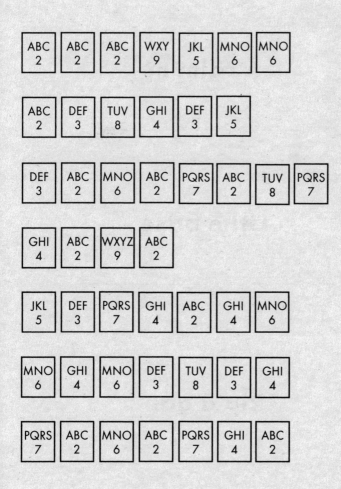

ABC 2	ABC 2	ABC 2	WXY 9	JKL 5	MNO 6	MNO 6

ABC 2	DEF 3	TUV 8	GHI 4	DEF 3	JKL 5

DEF 3	ABC 2	MNO 6	ABC 2	PQRS 7	ABC 2	TUV 8	PQRS 7

GHI 4	ABC 2	WXYZ 9	ABC 2

JKL 5	DEF 3	PQRS 7	GHI 4	ABC 2	GHI 4	MNO 6

MNO 6	GHI 4	MNO 6	DEF 3	TUV 8	DEF 3	GHI 4

PQRS 7	ABC 2	MNO 6	ABC 2	PQRS 7	GHI 4	ABC 2

BOOKS OF THE BIBLE. . .

A calm hi

_ _ _ _ _ _ _

WOMEN OF THE BIBLE. . .

Lithe base

_ _ _ _ _ _ _ _ _

KINGS. . .

Rip a gap

_ _ _ _ _ _ _

**Day
270**

GENESIS

GRADING	1,000	_____	1. ___ ___
VENISON	Climbing plants	_____	2. ___ ___
HUNDRED	Below	_____	3. ___ ___
CLAIMED	Award of honor	_____	4. ___ ___
FARMERS	Skeleton	_____	5. ___ ___
ELATION	Romance	_____	6. ___ ___
AWARDED	Fear	_____	7. ___ ___
WRITTEN	Correspond	_____	8. ___ ___
MISSILE	Becomes slender	_____	9. ___ ___
DAMMING	Urchin	_____	10. ___ ___
ABDOMEN	Studied	_____	11. ___ ___
EGGHEAD	Encircle	_____	12. ___ ___
NEAREST	Look fixedly	_____	13. ___ ___

___ ___ ___ ___ ___ ___ ___ ___ ___ ___ ___ ___ ___

___ ___ ___ ___ ___ ___ ___ ___ ___ ___ ___ ___ ___

1 2 3 4 5 6 7 8 9 10 11 12 13

1 Corinthians 9:24

	1	2	3	4	5
1	P	V	Q	C	R
2	W	D	M	S	O
3	G	Z	B	Y	I
4	U	J	F	H	N
5	T	L	E	K	A

54-45-25-21   34-53   45-25-51   51-44-55-51

51-44-53-34   21-44-35-14-44   15-41-45   35-45

55   15-55-14-53   15-41-45   55-52-52,   33-41-51

25-45-53   15-53-14-53-35-12-53-51-44   51-44-53

11-15-35-32-53?   24-25   15-41-45,   51-44-55-51

34-53   23-55-34   25-33-51-55-35-45.

1 Corinthians 12:13

A man's suit worn for a semi-formal or formal occasion

—— —— —— —— —— ——
11   39   20   2   26   35

A collection of rings, bracelets, or necklaces

—— —— —— —— —— —— ——
30   5   25   12   16   19   8

The branch of biology that studies animals

—— —— —— —— —— —— ——
29   36   4   24   33   15   38

Material

—— —— —— —— —— ——
32   3   21   13   7   6

A trail

—— —— —— ——
17   22   1   27

A ship that can operate underwater

—— —— —— —— —— —— —— —— ——
14   34   9   28   18   37   31   10   23

32-35-13   9-38   35-10-23   14-17-7-37-31-1

22-13-12   25-2   18-16-24   9-3-17-11-7-29-2-26

31-10-11-35   4-10-12   9-35-26-8,

25-27-5-1-27-23-13   25-12   21-2

30-12-25-14   35-13   15-2-10-11-7-16-12-14,

25-27-23-1-27-23-37   25-12   9-23   21-4-10-26

33-19   32-19-23-12.

Scrambled Circles

1. TEDEADCI
2. ETNWIRT
3. OGORNVRE
4. NESTARV
5. VREIR
6. GBNUIDLI
7. OPUN
8. OSENIDTI

This Roman coin was equivalent in weight to the Hebrew shekel.

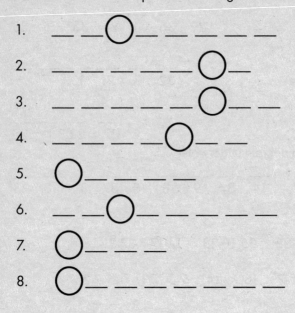

1. _ _ Ⓓ _ _ _ _ _
2. _ _ _ _ _ Ⓔ _
3. _ _ _ _ _ Ⓝ _ _
4. _ _ _ _ Ⓐ _ _
5. Ⓡ _ _ _ _
6. _ _ Ⓘ _ _ _ _ _
7. Ⓤ _ _ _
8. Ⓢ _ _ _ _ _ _ _

Answer: _ _ _ _ _ _ _ _

1. KW QUPWZEH ZYP DYRBSDI;
   KER SD WNWPG RBSDI KG
   CPUGWP UDF JECCHSQURSYD
   LSRB RBUDXJISNSDI HWR GYEP
   PWVEWJRJ KW TUFW XDYLD
   EDRY IYF.

2. ERYRNZ NH TMOR, ZMP PEGP
   KR TMORC XMC, LBP PEGP ER
   TMORC BH, GZC HRZP ENH
   HMZ PM LR PER VYMVNPNGPNMZ
   JMY MBY HNZH.

3. EAV WF XEGV QI QWFH ERR,
   GY EAO HEA JGRR PIHF EYQFB
   HF, RFQ WGH VFAO WGHXFRY,
   EAV QENF DM WGX PBIXX
   VEGRO, EAV YIRRIJ HF.

New Testament Headlines

1.

**TR●STED FRIEN●
BETR●Y● ●UST MAN**

— — — — —

2.

**KING ●PP●RENTLY
LISTENS TO ●RIS●NE●'S
●RIP●ING TEST●MONY**

— — — — — — — —

3.

**MA● COMM●●DED TO
B●PT●ZE ●N EX-PER●ECUTOR**

— — — — — — —

ROMANS 8:5

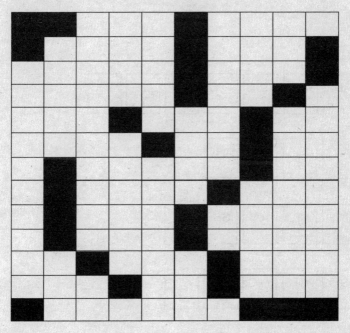

```
A   L   H   A   E   O   D   T   T   I
F   N   T   E   E   S   E   F   T   E
I   N   E   R   E   Y   F   T   B   M
I   G   D   L   E   F   A   T   H   H
E   F   A   H   R   I   S   R   E   H
T   T   T   I   T   H   T   H   E   E
T   S   G   O   R   E   A   P   E   U
R   T   S   T   R   O   T   H   I   R
I       P   S   R       H   O   T   A
N       F   S   H       T   H   H   Y
        F   H   T               H
        T       H
```

CHRIST FIGURES IN THE OLD TESTAMENT

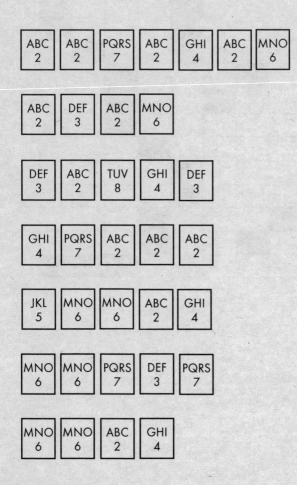

| ABC 2 | ABC 2 | PQRS 7 | ABC 2 | GHI 4 | ABC 2 | MNO 6 |

| ABC 2 | DEF 3 | ABC 2 | MNO 6 |

| DEF 3 | ABC 2 | TUV 8 | GHI 4 | DEF 3 |

| GHI 4 | PQRS 7 | ABC 2 | ABC 2 | ABC 2 |

| JKL 5 | MNO 6 | MNO 6 | ABC 2 | GHI 4 |

| MNO 6 | MNO 6 | PQRS 7 | DEF 3 | PQRS 7 |

| MNO 6 | MNO 6 | ABC 2 | GHI 4 |

BOOKS OF THE BIBLE. . .

So scan oils

_ _ _ _ _ _ _ _ _ _

WOMEN OF THE BIBLE. . .

Hail led

_ _ _ _ _ _ _

EVENTS. . .

Puts pearls

_ _ _ _   _ _ _ _ _ _

JOSHUA

GRAFTED	Swap	_____	1. ___ ___
PLATOON	Shrub	_____	2. ___ ___
DEAREST	Pester	_____	3. ___ ___
MARTIAL	Warning	_____	4. ___ ___
REFRESH	Allude	_____	5. ___ ___
WEATHER	Organ	_____	6. ___ ___
LITERAL	Not now	_____	7. ___ ___
STATION	Smooth cloth	_____	8. ___ ___
THROUGH	Strong	_____	9. ___ ___
TRACKED	Squeak	_____	10. ___ ___
FRESHET	Releases	_____	11. ___ ___
MESSIAH	Not right	_____	12. ___ ___
ELYSIAN	Murdered	_____	13. ___ ___

— — — — — — — — — — — — —

— — — — — — — — — — — — —

1   2   3   4   5   6   7   8   9   10   11   12   13

Ecclesiastes 3:1

	1	2	3	4	5
1	P	V	Q	C	R
2	W	D	M	S	O
3	G	Z	B	Y	I
4	U	J	F	H	N
5	T	L	E	K	A

51-25   53-12-53-15-34   51-44-35-45-31

51-44-53-15-53   35-24   55   24-53-55-24-25-45,

55-45-22   55   51-35-23-53   51-25   53-12-53-15-34

11-41-15-11-25-24-53   41-45-22-53-15   51-44-53

44-53-55-12-53-45.

1 Corinthians 10:33

A violent tropical storm with winds over 74 mph

—— —— —— —— —— —— —— —— ——
23 38 9 20 40 30 34 13 28

General good health and strength

—— —— —— —— —— —— ——
36 10 33 21 4 27 14

The use of charms or spells, supposedly to control events

—— —— —— —— ——
15 31 5 41 22

A light, purplish blue

—— —— —— —— —— —— —— —— —— ——
37 42 8 7 25 46 3 39 18 47

Open to criticism

—— —— —— —— —— —— —— —— —— ——
32 6 24 2 35 16 26 45 29 19

At a distance

—— —— —— —— —— ——
44 17 11 43 1 12

4-32-35-21   31-27   46   37-24-35-26-14-35

26-18-29   15-4-13   40-11   34-24-18

33-23-10-2-5-14,   3-17-33   27-4-28-39-41-21-5

15-41-21-47   17-25-13   37-20-17-36-10-33,   45-6-33

33-23-42   37-12-17-36-41-33   17-36   15-34-21-44,

33-23-31-33   33-23-19-44   15-26-44   45-28

27-31-32-4-43.

1. ELSETIV
2. EPRAVSOS
3. BALSM
4. ETRIBM
5. SRMA

6. URENBM
7. ASUDIR
8. CEERED
9. LIDKEL
10. VEESN

An outdoor shelter for holding religious services.

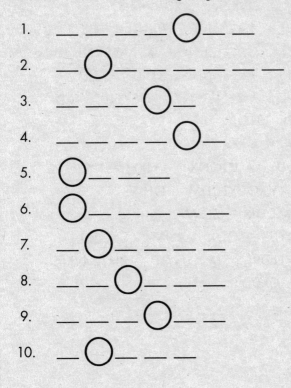

1. __ __ __ __ ◯ __ __

2. __ ◯ __ __ __ __ __ __

3. __ __ __ ◯ __

4. __ __ __ __ ◯ __

5. ◯ __ __ __

6. ◯ __ __ __ __ __

7. __ ◯ __ __ __ __

8. __ __ ◯ __ __ __

9. __ __ __ ◯ __ __

10. __ ◯ __ __ __

Answer: __ __ __ __ __ __ __ __ __ __

1. CAL   XWP   IGTL   YGL   VCRL   ZAXG
   XWP   QGDCA,   QWCX   RV   XWRV
   XWCX   XWGZ   WCVX   LGAP?   CAL
   XWP   QGDCA   VCRL,   XWP   VPTJPAX
   EPYZRIPL   DP,   CAL   R   LRL   PCX.

2. NIS   AKNISDH   HIKUU   JXN   GS
   ZEN   NX   OSKNI   AXD   NIS
   VIQUODSJ,   JSQNISD   HIKUU   NIS
   VIQUODSJ   GS   ZEN   NX   OSKNI
   AXD   NIS   AKNISDH: STSDF   CKJ
   HIKUU   GS   ZEN   NX   OSKNI   AXD
   IQH   XRJ   HQJ.

3. Q   CQDD   AUOQGX   VNXX;   KYU
   Q   OS   KXOUKLDDM   OHW
   CYHWXUKLDDM   SOWX:
   SOURXDDYLG   OUX   VNM   CYUZG;
   OHW   VNOV   SM   GYLD   ZHYCXVN
   UQBNV   CXDD.

New Testament Headlines

1.

**MAN WONDERS HOW
BOY'S LUNCH WILL FEED
A CROWD**

— —— —— —— — —

2.

**BROTHER PLANS FOR
WELL-BEING OF
DISCIPLE BROTHERS**

— —— —— —— — ——

3.

**WOMAN DOES INSTANTLY
FOR LYING INCOME AND
KEEPING PART OF PROCEEDS**

— —— —— —— —— — ——

**Day
285**

PSALM 91:2

```
R    O    R    E    I    U    I    S    L    Y
N    D    I    M    E    H    G    E    U    O
I    L    L    S    F    L    F    R    R    M
T    D    W    I    L    M    I    S    A    A
I    E    F    N    T    H    T    O    G    T
R         S    H    Y    H    E    M         O
D                        E    Y              W
                                             S
```

GOD IS. . .

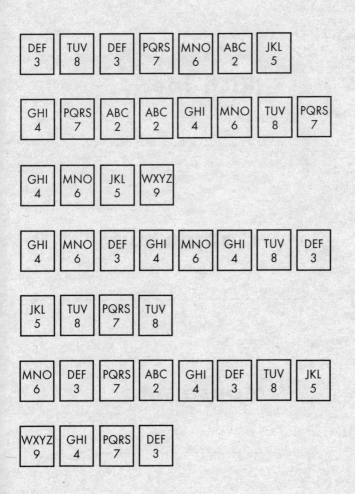

BIBLE CITIES. . . .

Rich Joe

— — — — — — —

BAD GUYS. . .

Into apple suit

— — — — — —   — — — — — —

NEW TESTAMENT PEOPLE. . .

Mouse sin

— — — — — — — —

Haggai

ANEROID	Bee	_____	1. ___ ___
IMPASTO	Jazz dance	_____	2. ___ ___
MIGRANT	Wood fiber	_____	3. ___ ___
WEATHER	Consumer	_____	4. ___ ___
INDITED	Supped	_____	5. ___ ___
CHAPLET	Put	_____	6. ___ ___
HYDRATE	Late	_____	7. ___ ___
LEPROSY	Literary medium	_____	8. ___ ___
ROOTAGE	Rasp	_____	9. ___ ___
TOURISM	Damp	_____	10. ___ ___
SHORTED	Pain	_____	11. ___ ___

__ __ __ __ __ __ __ __ __ __ __

__ __ __ __ __ __ __ __ __ __ __

1 2 3 4 5 6 7 8 9 10 11

Romans 12:10

33-31   21-13-12-44-41-23

11-32-32-31-25-51-13-14-12-31-44   14-12-31   51-14

11-12-14-51-22-31-15   54-13-51-22

33-15-14-51-22-31-15-41-23   41-14-45-31;

13-12   22-14-12-14-52-15

55-15-31-32-31-15-15-13-12-53   14-12-31

11-12-14-51-22-31-15.

1 Corinthians 6:12

One's natural disposition

$\overline{}$ $\overline{}$ $\overline{}$ $\overline{}$ $\overline{}$ $\overline{}$ $\overline{}$ $\overline{}$ $\overline{}$ $\overline{}$ $\overline{}$
39 16 37 11 25 28 1 19 33 24 45

More than accounted for

$\overline{}$ $\overline{}$ $\overline{}$ $\overline{}$ $\overline{}$
43 6 15 2 38

Wailed, as wolves

$\overline{}$ $\overline{}$ $\overline{}$ $\overline{}$ $\overline{}$ $\overline{}$
34 29 10 20 44 5

Protective gear for a rainy day

$\overline{}$ $\overline{}$ $\overline{}$ $\overline{}$ $\overline{}$ $\overline{}$ $\overline{}$ $\overline{}$
12 27 3 31 21 40 17 8

Relating to an overall plan

$\overline{}$ $\overline{}$ $\overline{}$ $\overline{}$ $\overline{}$ $\overline{}$ $\overline{}$ $\overline{}$ $\overline{}$
41 13 30 4 22 18 7 36 26

A second-person singular pronoun

$\overline{}$ $\overline{}$ $\overline{}$ $\overline{}$ $\overline{}$ $\overline{}$ $\overline{}$ $\overline{}$
32 46 14 47 9 35 23 42

4-40-20   39-34-36-24-7-41   38-47-25

20-38-10-42-12-23   12-24-15-29   19-21,   3-12-45

1-40-20   15-34-36-24-7-41   8-2-35   24-29-22

43-6-11-18-5-36-18-24-45;   1-20-23   15-34-36-24-7-9

4-30-35   17-38-10-42-14-23   42-29-31   27-33,

3-12-22   36   10-36-17-40   24-29-13   3-43

3-2-29-12-7-34-15   12-24-5-21-47   13-34-16

11-46-10-44-28   29–42   38-24-32.

1. ICTUB
2. SPHUBIL
3. NPEI
4. GBRTHOU
5. DIIVDE

6. RASWET
7. NPSOROIT
8. PEYTG
9. ERDEVIG

The job of a high government official.

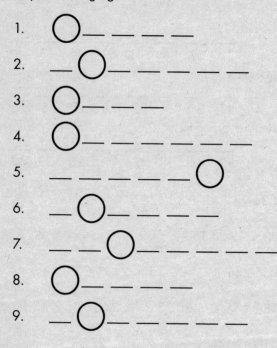

1. ◯ _ _ _ _
2. _ ◯ _ _ _ _ _
3. ◯ _ _ _
4. ◯ _ _ _ _ _
5. _ _ _ _ _ ◯
6. _ ◯ _ _ _
7. _ _ ◯ _ _ _ _ _
8. ◯ _ _ _ _
9. _ ◯ _ _ _ _

Answer: _ _ _ _ _ _ _ _ _ _ _

1. VUP NLLJPNVBJAM BFJ VUQJA IX
   BFJ AIKP WLIBJ FNL, DJZVEWJ
   FJ QVGJ UIB QIP BFJ QAIKM:
   VUP FJ OVW JVBJU IX OIKLW,
   VUP QVGJ EC BFJ QFIWB.

2. JDY BGZ AZQUDFP DJ DXY
   AQYJQYZ QYZ FDB OQYFQH, EXB
   TVRGBN BGYDXRG RDC BD BGZ
   UXHHVFR CDAF DJ PBYDFR
   GDHCP.

3. AU MANM DYRUEUMA AJI IJHI
   IANOO HYM VEYIVUE: TBM
   XAYIY DYHWUIIUMA NHL
   WYEINCUMA MAUG IANOO ANRU
   GUEDS.

New Testament Headlines

1.

MAN HO●ELESSLY ●RI●S TO ERO●E B●AME W●TH HAND WASHING

— — — — — —

2.

J●SUS C●LLED ●AX COLLEC●OR TO FOLLO● ●I●

— — — — — — —

3.

S●ORT T●X ●OLLE●TOR H●S ●ESTFULLY RET●RNED ●TOL●N GOODS

— — — — — — — —

PROVERBS 2:6

New Testament People with God-Given Missions

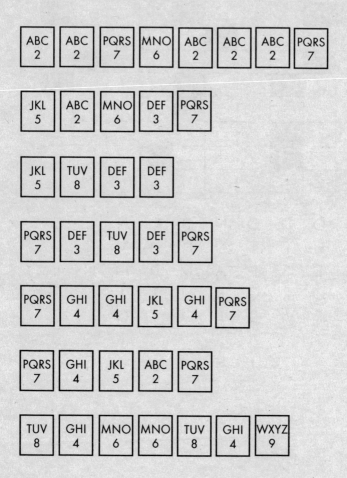

ABC 2	ABC 2	PQRS 7	MNO 6	ABC 2	ABC 2	ABC 2	PQRS 7

JKL 5	ABC 2	MNO 6	DEF 3	PQRS 7

JKL 5	TUV 8	DEF 3	DEF 3

PQRS 7	DEF 3	TUV 8	DEF 3	PQRS 7

PQRS 7	GHI 4	GHI 4	JKL 5	GHI 4	PQRS 7

PQRS 7	GHI 4	JKL 5	ABC 2	PQRS 7

TUV 8	GHI 4	MNO 6	MNO 6	TUV 8	GHI 4	WXYZ 9

Day
296

BOOKS OF THE BIBLE. . .

She is a pen

— — — — — — — — —

EVENTS. . .

Sap roves

— — — — — — —

BOOKS OF THE BIBLE. . .

Burns me

— — — — — —

LUKE

MICHAEL	Blood sucker	_____	1. __ __
ARCHAIC	Official seat	_____	2. __ __
GRENADE	Incline	_____	3. __ __
ASHTRAY	Waste	_____	4. __ __
FASTEST	Banquet	_____	5. __ __
HEATHEN	Devoured	_____	6. __ __
AVARICE	Slice turkey	_____	7. __ __
LARGEST	Elaborate	_____	8. __ __
BEASTLY	Leaven	_____	9. __ __
REPLICA	Arrange	_____	10. __ __
ENSURED	Sand hills	_____	11. __ __
JESTING	Scorch	_____	12. __ __
DEBOUCH	Diced	_____	13. __ __

__ __ __ __ __ __ __ __ __ __ __ __ __

__ __ __ __ __ __ __ __ __ __ __ __ __

1 2 3 4 5 6 7 8 9 10 11 12 13

Psalm 25:7

	1	2	3	4	5
1	A	N	I	O	R
2	K	H	Y	S	C
3	E	F	B	M	Q
4	L	J	Z	D	V
5	T	U	G	W	P

15-31-34-31-34-33-31-15   12-14-51   51-22-31

24-13-12-24   14-32   34-23   23-14-52-51-22,   12-14-15

34-23   51-15-11-12-24-53-15-31-24-24-13-14-12-24:

11-25-25-14-15-44-13-12-53   51-14   51-22-23

34-31-15-25-23   15-31-34-31-34-33-31-15   51-22-14-52

34-31   32-14-15   51-22-23   53-14-14-44-12-31-24-24-24'

24-11-21-31,   14   41-14-15-44.

Acrostic

1 CORINTHIANS 4:10

Appropriate for the occasion

$\overline{42}$ $\overline{11}$ $\overline{27}$ $\overline{5}$ $\overline{21}$ $\overline{35}$ $\overline{15}$ $\overline{29}$

Polite

$\overline{17}$ $\overline{30}$ $\overline{9}$ $\overline{26}$ $\overline{34}$ $\overline{3}$ $\overline{36}$ $\overline{14}$ $\overline{20}$

To grow in number (adverb)

$\overline{44}$ $\overline{10}$ $\overline{37}$ $\overline{4}$ $\overline{41}$ $\overline{16}$ $\overline{31}$ $\overline{8}$ $\overline{39}$ $\overline{13}$ $\overline{25}$ $\overline{33}$

Having much depth

$\overline{22}$ $\overline{18}$ $\overline{28}$ $\overline{2}$

A crisp batter cake with small, square hollows

$\overline{40}$ $\overline{1}$ $\overline{12}$ $\overline{23}$ $\overline{6}$ $\overline{32}$

An almond color used to describe pants

$\overline{24}$ $\overline{38}$ $\overline{7}$ $\overline{19}$ $\overline{43}$

40-29   21-26-41   12-30-36-25-20   23-30-26

37-38-26-43-20-34-'20   20-7-19-32,   35-11-34

33-3   21-26-41   40-8-31-3   27-10

17-38-26-44-31-34;   40-32   21-26-41   40-3-21-24,

35-14-34   33-3   16-4-41   20-34-26-36-10-13;

33-18   1-4-28   38-30-39-36-9-4-16-35-15-3,

35-14-5   40-29   16-4-29   22-28-31-2-43-20-29-22.

Scrambled Circles

1. SOPORT
2. NEAVEH
3. HASVIN
4. REEDVLI
5. NETVEID
6. TMIMOC
7. SOSESPS
8. NDEIRCS

A letter was written to this believer, the master of a runaway slave.

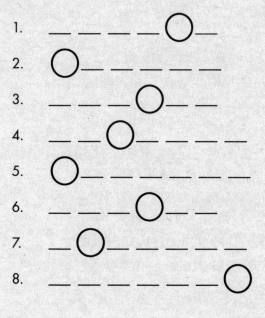

1. __ __ __ __ ◯ __

2. ◯ __ __ __ __ __

3. __ __ __ ◯ __ __

4. __ __ ◯ __ __ __

5. ◯ __ __ __ __ __ __

6. __ __ __ ◯ __ __

7. __ ◯ __ __ __ __ __

8. __ __ __ __ __ __ ◯

Answer: __ __ __ __ __ __ __ __

1. SOQ XW LVVP KYWSQ, SOQ BSRW
   LXSOPG, SOQ KYSPW HL, SOQ
   BSRW COLV LXWJ, GSEHOB,
   LXHG HG JE KVQE IXHFX HG
   BHRWO NVY EVC: LXHG QV HO
   YWJWJKYSOFW VN JW.

2. RI YE LBXPJQ'Z PKVZJ BQJ YBIE
   YBIZRKIZ: RL RX AJQJ IKX ZK,
   R AKVWH PBTJ XKWH EKV. R
   NK XK MQJMBQJ B MWBFJ LKQ
   EKV.

3. APZ RFX XHXW PA RFX YPZS
   ZKE RP DES AZP RFZPKNFPKR
   RFX UFPYX XDZRF, RP WFXU
   FTGWXYA WRZPEN TE RFX
   QXFDYA PA RFXG UFPWX FXDZR
   TW VXZAXLR RPUDZS FTG.

New Testament Headlines

1.

RULER M●S●●KES JE●US FOR DE●D ●RISO●ER

— — — — — — —

2.

●AN IN CROWD FORCED TO HELP PR●●●●ER CARRY HIS CROSS

— — — — —

3.

JES●S ●●KES ●HE ●L●ND BEGG●● ●E●

— — — — — — — — —

ROMANS 8:37

```
    S   U   T   N   L   L   N   G   O   D
W   O   E   A   H   I   H   M   O   E
E   H   S   T   R   E   O   V   T   N
R   N   U   A   O   L   S   T   H   H
T   E   A   H   H   R       I   S   R
I   U       R   A   N       C   M
Q   E       G   A   Y       E
                T
```

BOOKS OF THE NEW TESTAMENT

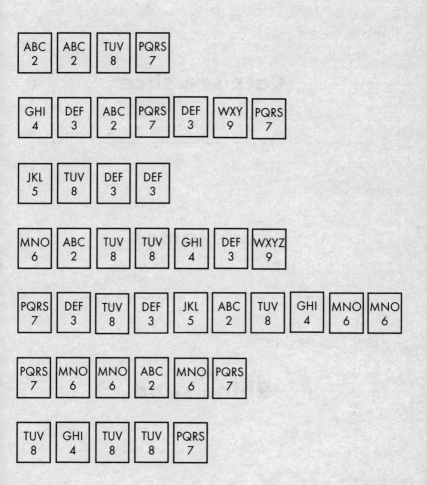

| ABC 2 | ABC 2 | TUV 8 | PQRS 7 |

| GHI 4 | DEF 3 | ABC 2 | PQRS 7 | DEF 3 | WXY 9 | PQRS 7 |

| JKL 5 | TUV 8 | DEF 3 | DEF 3 |

| MNO 6 | ABC 2 | TUV 8 | TUV 8 | GHI 4 | DEF 3 | WXYZ 9 |

| PQRS 7 | DEF 3 | TUV 8 | DEF 3 | JKL 5 | ABC 2 | TUV 8 | GHI 4 | MNO 6 | MNO 6 |

| PQRS 7 | MNO 6 | MNO 6 | ABC 2 | MNO 6 | PQRS 7 |

| TUV 8 | GHI 4 | TUV 8 | TUV 8 | PQRS 7 |

Books of the Bible. . .

Cats see slice

_ _ _ _ _ _ _ _ _ _ _ _ _

Bible Cities. . .

Rule James

_ _ _ _ _ _ _ _ _

New Testament People. . .

Rhine sand

_ _ _ _ _ _ _ _ _

Romans 14:9

A person from another country

<u> </u> <u> </u> <u> </u> <u> </u> <u> </u> <u> </u> <u> </u> <u> </u> <u> </u>
26 42 33 5 35 12 4 23 18

The month after September

<u> </u> <u> </u> <u> </u> <u> </u> <u> </u> <u> </u> <u> </u>
32 40 6 47 43 13 36

A daytime performance

<u> </u> <u> </u> <u> </u> <u> </u> <u> </u> <u> </u> <u> </u>
44 20 14 41 1 37 31

Vindictive

<u> </u> <u> </u> <u> </u> <u> </u> <u> </u> <u> </u> <u> </u> <u> </u>
34 39 3 27 22 17 7 28

Not seen

<u> </u> <u> </u> <u> </u> <u> </u> <u> </u> <u> </u>
2 21 11 29 24 16

Incapable of occurring

<u> </u> <u> </u> <u> </u> <u> </u> <u> </u> <u> </u> <u> </u> <u> </u> <u> </u> <u> </u>
25 45 10 19 15 8 9 46 38 30

26-32-36   6-19   14-2-35-15   13-1-11

40-2-18-21-15-6   43-32-14-2   11-25-23-11,

20-1-11   36-47-8-30,   20-4-11   18-24-34-9-34-22-11,

6-2-20-6   2-5   44-35-27-2-6   43-37   28-19-33-11

46-32-6-2   42-17   14-2-39   11-31-20-11

20-3-29   38-25-34-41-16-12.

1. TOTNNEC
2. WASROR
3. GSONIST
4. ELOMOASTH

5. HODLCET
6. MOROCTF
7. NREUTR
8. DESRRWA

A method that ancient pagans used to determine the future.

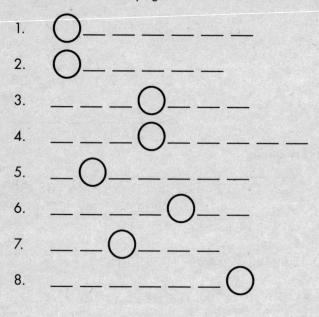

1. ◯__ __ __ __ __ __
2. ◯__ __ __ __ __
3. __ __ __ ◯__ __ __
4. __ __ __ ◯__ __ __ __ __
5. __ ◯__ __ __ __ __
6. __ __ __ ◯__ __
7. __ __ ◯__ __ __
8. __ __ __ __ __ __ ◯

Answer: __ __ __ __   __ __ __ __

1. NSK FWJ CRTNS MNOJ N GRS,
   NSK LNUUJK WXG SNTJ GNTGRS:
   NSK FWJ LWXUK HOJC, NSK
   FWJ UROK MUJGGJK WXT.

2. EU ET NR UVH WNIK'T ZHILEHT
   UVPU CH PIH QNU LNQTGZHK,
   OHLPGTH VET LNZMPTTENQT
   RPEW QNU. UVHX PIH QHC
   HFHIX ZNIQEQS: SIHPU ET UVX
   RPEUVRGWQHTT.

3. YWF PKNJ TVWWUI EW LYRLP
   RSFI QJLUW, TWLTKXWM RSFI
   TLYF, FILF PW GLP OXKR IKR
   PW KNQIF FK LXTRWJ WBWJP
   GLX.

Hebrews

NESTLED	Horse	_____	1. __ __
CLOAKED	Encrusted	_____	2. __ __
LAWLESS	Bargains	_____	3. __ __
ATTIRED	Tire mark	_____	4. __ __
SEVENTH	Nervous	_____	5. __ __
FEELING	Throw	_____	6. __ __
JOBLESS	Bottoms	_____	7. __ __
PIOUSLY	Ruin	_____	8. __ __
FELSITE	Choice	_____	9. __ __
PAINTED	Yearned	_____	10. __ __
APHESIS	Form	_____	11. __ __
BROTHER	Ship worm	_____	12. __ __
ASHAMED	Women	_____	13. __ __

__ __ __ __ __ __ __ __ __ __ __ __ __

__ __ __ __ __ __ __ __ __ __ __ __ __

1   2   3   4   5   6   7   8   9   10   11   12   13

Romans 12:10

	1	2	3	4	5
1	A	N	I	O	R
2	K	H	Y	S	C
3	E	F	B	M	Q
4	L	J	Z	D	V
5	T	U	G	W	P

33-31   21-13-12-44-41-23

11-32-32-31-25-51-13-14-12-31-44   14-12-31   51-14

11-12-14-51-22-31-15   54-13-51-22   33-15-14-51-22-31-15-41-23;

41-14-45-31:   13-12   22-14-12-14-52-15

55-15-31-32-31-15-15-13-12-53   14-12-31

11-12-14-51-22-31-15

ROMANS 14:11

Appropriate

___ ___ ___ ___ ___
11 33   6 29 23

One who follows Jesus

___ ___ ___ ___ ___ ___ ___ ___ ___
22 28 10 43 38 15 34   1 21

A sport played with clubs and tees

___ ___ ___ ___
16   7 27 37

Generous welcome

___ ___ ___ ___ ___ ___ ___ ___ ___ ___ ___
44   2   5 12 14 30 41   8 24 35 18

The exercise with routine

___ ___ ___ ___ ___ ___ ___
17 42 25   3 39 31 20

An instrument used measuring atmospheric pressure

___ ___ ___ ___ ___ ___ ___ ___ ___
26 13 45 36   4 19   9 40 32

37-2-32   14-15   34-38   17-10-34-15-9-19-21,

33-5   29   27-34-11-19,   38-41-43-9-28   15-28-19

27-7-10-23,   19-11-40-45-18   3-21-40-19

38-28-33-6-27   26-2-17   20-36   4-40,   1-21-23

40-11-19-25-18   15-36-21-16-31-19   38-44-13-6-27

22-39-21-37-19-5-38   15-42   16-36-23.

Scrambled Circles

1. EPRESREV
2. NGIHIERL
3. UOETNG
4. NIMEGIA
5. OSNEKT
6. WHTRA
7. ACEREDL
8. EISNCAER
9. LWNBO
10. RAENG

Pressed into wax to seal important documents.

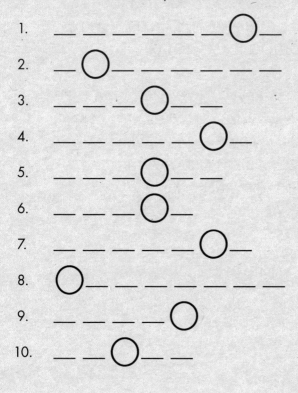

1. __ __ __ __ __ __ ◯ __
2. __ ◯ __ __ __ __ __ __
3. __ __ __ ◯ __ __
4. __ __ __ __ ◯ __
5. __ __ __ ◯ __ __
6. __ __ __ ◯ __
7. __ __ __ __ __ ◯ __
8. ◯ __ __ __ __ __ __ __
9. __ __ __ __ ◯
10. __ __ ◯ __ __

Answer: __ __ __ __ __ __   __ __ __ __

1. CORARQXAR URNWP MDBCNQNRS UH QVNCO, FR OVER YRVTR FNCO PXS COAXDPO XDA KXAS MRBDB TOANBC.

2. SXDBD DJTY BICH UXE, T JP CUX EXDBEEXZCTHI, JIY CUX QTWX: UX CUJC KXQTXAXCU TI PX, CUHBVU UX LXEX YXJY, NXC DUJQQ UX QTAX.

3. YKJBAOO RKVN BWVHPO KJA PK WJKPDAN, WJZ LNWR KJA BKN WJKPDAN, PDWP RA IWR XA DAWHAZ. PDA ABBAYPVWH BANUAJP LNWRAN KB W NECDPAKVO IWJ WUWEHAPD IVYD.

NEW TESTAMENT HEADLINES

1.

●U●T MAN T● WED
●IS ●REGNANT FIANC●E

— — — — — —

2.

AGGR●VATED SISTER
●ORE CONCERNED ABOUT
CHO●ES TH●N WI●H ●ER GUEST

— — — — — —

3.

PERSECUTED JEWISH CHR●STI●N
FLEES ITA●Y ●●ICKLY AND
ASSISTS ●POSTLE

— — — — — —

1 CORINTHIANS 10:31

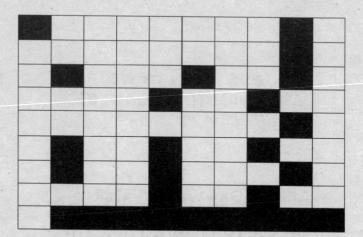

```
H   W   R   K   E   V   R   R   A   T
E   O   E   O   F   D   O   E   W   Y
R   I   N   O   T   H   R   R   G   D
A   E   S   O   T   O   E   R       D
E   T   T   O   T   T   F   E       G
L       R   E   O       O           O
L       H   Y   O       H           Y
D       D   A           H           H
                                    L
```

ANIMALS IN THE NEW TESTAMENT

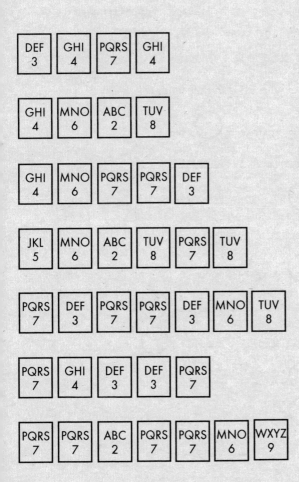

| DEF 3 | GHI 4 | PQRS 7 | GHI 4 | | | |

| GHI 4 | MNO 6 | ABC 2 | TUV 8 | | | |

| GHI 4 | MNO 6 | PQRS 7 | PQRS 7 | DEF 3 | | |

| JKL 5 | MNO 6 | ABC 2 | TUV 8 | PQRS 7 | TUV 8 | |

| PQRS 7 | DEF 3 | PQRS 7 | PQRS 7 | DEF 3 | MNO 6 | TUV 8 |

| PQRS 7 | GHI 4 | DEF 3 | DEF 3 | PQRS 7 | | |

| PQRS 7 | PQRS 7 | ABC 2 | PQRS 7 | PQRS 7 | MNO 6 | WXYZ 9 |

Scrambled Circles

1. SOPORT
2. TESVARH
3. KICEDW
4. SILE
5. NIEW
6. BERBORS

7. TONSENC
8. TISDM
9. WNOK
10. REROMF
11. ROSU

Enemies of Israel who lived in Palestine.

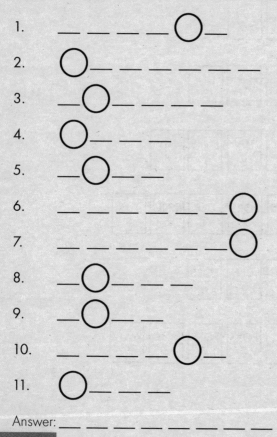

1. __ __ __ __ 〇 __
2. 〇 __ __ __ __ __ __
3. __ 〇 __ __ __ __
4. 〇 __ __ __
5. __ 〇 __ __
6. __ __ __ __ __ 〇
7. __ __ __ __ __ __ 〇
8. __ 〇 __ __ __
9. __ 〇 __ __
10. __ __ __ 〇 __
11. 〇 __ __ __

Answer: __ __ __ __ __ __ __ __ __ __ __

BOOKS OF THE BIBLE. . .

A voter line

_ _ _ _ _ _ _ _ _ _

WOMEN OF THE BIBLE. . .

Her beak

_ _ _ _ _ _ _

PLACES. . .

Doe can aim

_ _ _ _ _ _ _ _ _ _

Drop Two

MALACHI

REFRACT	Respond	_____ 1. __ __
EARSHOT	Garbage	_____ 2. __ __
OURSELF	Bad person	_____ 3. __ __
HOLBEIN	Aristocrat	_____ 4. __ __
NEPOTIC	Theme	_____ 5. __ __
SALIENT	Angle	_____ 6. __ __
RASPING	Mimicking	_____ 7. __ __
MILDEST	Kept watch	_____ 8. __ __
DEFICIT	Quoted	_____ 9. __ __
IRKSOME	Code	_____ 10. __ __
SPRAYER	Beseeches	_____ 11. __ __
PAINTER	Block letters	_____ 12. __ __

— — — — — — — — — — — —

— — — — — — — — — — — —

1 2 3 4 5 6 7 8 9 10 11 12

Day 320

Psalm 9:2

	1	2	3	4	5
1	A	N	I	O	R
2	K	H	Y	S	C
3	E	F	B	M	Q
4	L	J	Z	D	V
5	T	U	G	W	P

13   54-13-41-41 . 33-31   53-41-11-44   11-12-44

15-31-42-14-13-25-31   13-12   51-22-31-31:   13

54-13-41-41   24-13-12-53   55-15-11-13-24-31

51-14   51-22-23   12-11-34-31,   14   51-22-14-52

34-14-24-51   22-13-53-22.

Acrostic

1 Corinthians 6:15

Cold and unfeeling

$\overline{}$ $\overline{}$ $\overline{}$ $\overline{}$ $\overline{}$ $\overline{}$ $\overline{}$ $\overline{}$ $\overline{}$ $\overline{}$
30   14   43   7   31   25   18   38   2   48

Relating to the sense of smell

21   29   8   35   13   1   42   26   16

Cookout

39   19   46   6   34   28   44   12

When the sun rises

24   9   3   37

Plural for a male ruler of a monarchy

41   4   33   10   23

Based on an assumption

17   36   40   5   45   20   11   32   27   15   22   47

41-37-18-3   16-12   33-21-1   45-17-2-32

36-5-44-31   39-21-24-27-11-23   19-31-34   1-17-34

14-7-14-39-11-31-25   21-8   13-20-31-30-25-45?

25-20-22-48-47   4   45-17-34-37   1-35-41-12

45-20-12   14-34-14-6-7-31-25   21-8

15-17-31-27-25-45,   9-37-24   14-19-41-7   1-17-7-14

45-20-7   14-12-14-39-34-46-25   5-8   2-33

17-22-31-29-21-1?   10-42-24   8-21-26-6-30-24.

1. YPUTIR   5. TRSTU
2. ANEHTS   6. TOHMU
3. CYTAIPVTI   7. HESPIR
4. YNDEE

A tall plant that grows in swamps and rivers and is used to make heavy paper.

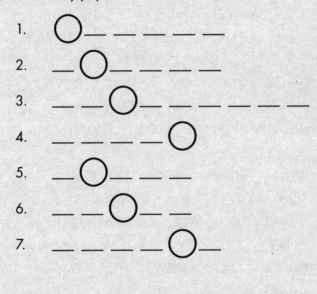

1. ◯__ __ __ __ __
2. __ ◯__ __ __ __
3. __ __ ◯__ __ __ __ __ __
4. __ __ __ __ ◯
5. __ ◯__ __ __
6. __ __ ◯__ __
7. __ __ __ __ ◯__

Answer: __ __ __ __ __ __ __

1. OFH MR SNT ANF, AQ HGNFEGH
   QXUC MEMUPRH ZQ; OFH ENK
   ZQMPH UH FPHN ENNK, HN
   OTUPE HN BMRR, MR UH UR HGUR
   KMA, HN RMXQ ZFDG BQNBCQ
   MCUXQ.

2. YXS VG WFWZP NEFEXA DCEXA
   VG YNN GNWHC, DKV VG WFWZP
   HVZD HCYND DCVB UZEXA
   EXDV DCW YZL, DV LWWT DCWO
   YNEFW KEDC DCWW; DCWP
   HCYNN UW OYNW YXS GWOYNW.

3. KYZ WCR UQBZ NRYW XRAQBR
   WCRI XV ZKV MY K JMUUKB
   QA K EUQDZ, WQ URKZ WCRI
   WCR NKV; KYZ XV YMTCW XY
   K JMUUKB QA AMBR, WQ TMSR
   WCRI UMTCW; WQ TQ XV ZKV
   KYZ YMTCW.

NEW TESTAMENT HEADLINES

1.

**TIRE● MISS●ON●RIES
GRACIOUSL● HOUSED
BY WOMAN SE●LER**

— — — — —

2.

**MAN PROM●TED BY
UNSEEN HO●Y S●IRIT TO
W●TNESS TO AN ET●IOP●AN**

— — — — — —

3.

**H●MBLE MAN WR●TES DOWN
●VERY WORD OF ●OMANS
WHILE APO●●LE DIC●ATES**

— — — — — — —

**Day
325**

HEBREWS 11:1

```
H   P   O   O   A   T   O   A   I   O
U   E   N   S   I   N   D   E   N   H
F   B   I   T   T   I   H   E   E   T
H       N   H   W   T   S   S   N   C
E       T   F   V   N   F   R       T
S       S   O       F   H   E       S
O       E   D           C   I       G
            E           G   E       N
```

OLD TESTAMENT PEOPLE
WITH GOD-GIVEN MISSIONS

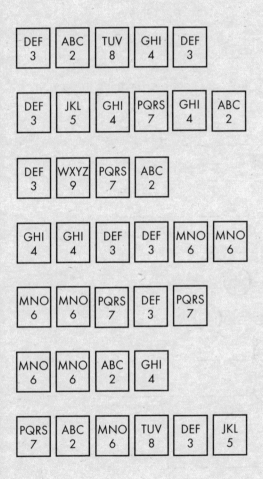

DEF 3	ABC 2	TUV 8	GHI 4	DEF 3

DEF 3	JKL 5	GHI 4	PQRS 7	GHI 4	ABC 2

DEF 3	WXYZ 9	PQRS 7	ABC 2

GHI 4	GHI 4	DEF 3	DEF 3	MNO 6	MNO 6

MNO 6	MNO 6	PQRS 7	DEF 3	PQRS 7

MNO 6	MNO 6	ABC 2	GHI 4

PQRS 7	ABC 2	MNO 6	TUV 8	DEF 3	JKL 5

Scrambled Circles

1. TSNERAV
2. NETURR
3. DARBACKW
4. RSDHEPEH
5. YANITV

6. THSUO
7. TULIB
8. HOSOIFL
9. ONWD
10. GPNSRI

Rules made by people that may not have anything to do with God's requirements.

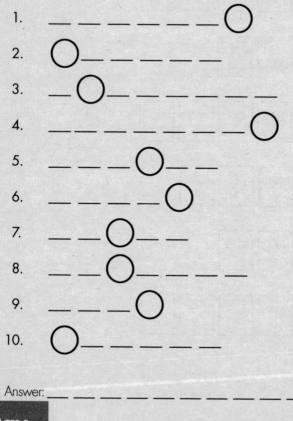

1. __ __ __ __ __ __ ◯
2. ◯ __ __ __ __ __
3. __ ◯ __ __ __ __ __ __
4. __ __ __ __ __ __ __ ◯
5. __ __ __ ◯ __ __
6. __ __ __ __ ◯
7. __ __ ◯ __ __
8. __ __ ◯ __ __ __ __
9. __ __ __ ◯
10. ◯ __ __ __ __ __

Answer: __ __ __ __ __ __ __ __ __ __

1. NLWGZF, EWGK HAE SHBA, UI
ZGOL; NLWGZF, EWGK HAE SHBA;
EWGK WHYE FGOLY' LILY
CBEWBQ EWI ZGRJY: EWI WHBA
BY HY H SZGRJ GS DGHEY,
EWHE HMMLHA SAGU UGKQE
DBZLHF.

2. ETR BNU MUWWUA BNEB NU
VERU QI LAEH JEW VEYYUR CT
BNU NETR QI BNU DQBBUY: WQ
NU VERU CB EXECT ETQBNUY
MUWWUA, EW WUUVUR XQQR BQ
BNU DQBBUY BQ VEOU CB.

3. QPWUHM PWEIHLHQ PWQ EPUQ,
KMHEEHQ KH VJH WPSH AO
BAQ OAL HRHL PWQ HRHL: OAL
IUEQAS PWQ SUBJV PLH JUE.

BIBLE CITIES. . .

Dooms

— — — — — —

KINGS. . .

Race hen and buzz

— — — — — — — — — — — — — —

EVENTS. . .

Star of grain unit

— — — — — — — — — — — — — —

Day 330

1 CORINTHIANS

CREATED	Step	_____	1. __ __
SPRIGHT	Seizes	_____	2. __ __
HEARTED	Cornered	_____	3. __ __
WESTERN	Sugary	_____	4. __ __
NAIROBI	Intellect	_____	5. __ __
TRANSIT	Pours	_____	6. __ __
YORKIST	Big bird	_____	7. __ __
THRIVED	Employed	_____	8. __ __
ANGELUS	Thrust	_____	9. __ __
UNAIRED	Draw off	_____	10. __ __
NET BALL	Furniture	_____	11. __ __
FITNESS	Trigonometric formula	_____	12. __ __

__ __ __ __ __ __ __ __ __ __ __ __

__ __ __ __ __ __ __ __ __ __ __ __

1 2 3 4 5 6 7 8 9 10 11 12

1 Corinthians 3:18

	1	2	3	4	5
1	A	N	I	O	R
2	K	H	Y	S	C
3	E	F	B	M	Q
4	L	J	Z	D	V
5	T	U	G	W	P

41-31-51   12-14   34-11-12   44-31-25-31-13-45-31

22-13-34-24-31-41-32.   13-32   11-12-23   34-11-12

11-34-14-12-53   23-14-52   24-31-31-34-31-51-22

51-14   33-31   54-13-24-31   13-12   51-22-13-24

54-14-15-41-44,   41-31-51   22-13-34

33-31-25-14-34-31   11   32-14-14-41,   51-22-11-51

22-31   34-11-23   33-31   54-13-24-31.

1 CORINTHIANS 5:8

A purposeful exaggeration

$\overline{33}$ $\overline{21}$ $\overline{8}$ $\overline{39}$ $\overline{15}$ $\overline{10}$ $\overline{31}$ $\overline{1}$ $\overline{26}$

Something regarded with a special liking

$\overline{20}$ $\overline{44}$ $\overline{7}$ $\overline{34}$ $\overline{25}$ $\overline{16}$ $\overline{12}$ $\overline{40}$

Bright red

$\overline{49}$ $\overline{17}$ $\overline{41}$ $\overline{32}$ $\overline{24}$ $\overline{6}$ $\overline{46}$

Exchanging information or talk

$\overline{38}$ $\overline{22}$ $\overline{47}$ $\overline{3}$ $\overline{43}$ $\overline{9}$ $\overline{35}$ $\overline{27}$ $\overline{13}$ $\overline{5}$ $\overline{30}$ $\overline{45}$ $\overline{18}$

To move on foot

$\overline{29}$ $\overline{36}$ $\overline{2}$ $\overline{14}$

Bought

$\overline{48}$ $\overline{19}$ $\overline{23}$ $\overline{4}$ $\overline{37}$ $\overline{28}$ $\overline{11}$ $\overline{42}$ $\overline{50}$

12-33-40-32-6-20-34-32-6   24-26-5   43-49

14-42-6-8   12-37-42   20-6-44-11-46,   9-45-12

29-16-12-33   31-1-50   2-42-28-7-6-9,

18-40-16-46-33-40-32   29-35-5-37   5-37-42

2-40-44-7-39-9   45-20   47-28-2-35-38-42   44-18-50

29-16-17-14-6-50-18-39-49-11;   10-43-46   29-35-12-33

5-37-42   43-9-24-40-41-7-26-9-39-50   10-25-39-44-50

22-20   49-16-18-27-39-15-30-5-21   36-9-50

46-23-19-5-37.

Scrambled Circles

1. NUEBDR
2. EMSROHTO
3. WRNDA
4. DATENT
5. FACECIISR
6. YEDOSRT
7. RUETTB
8. RANDEW
9. TECIED
10. SEENIEM

Special words from Jesus on the Mount of Olives.

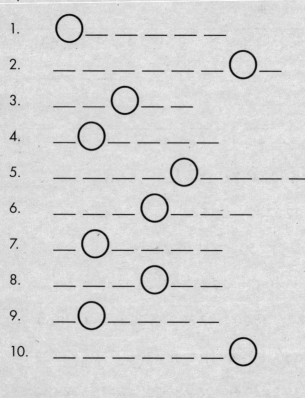

1. ◯— — — — —

2. — — — — — — ◯—

3. — — ◯— —

4. —◯— — — —

5. — — — —◯— — — —

6. — —◯— — —

7. —◯— — — —

8. — — —◯— —

9. —◯— — — —

10. — — — — — —◯

Answer: __ __ __ __ __ __ __ __ __ __

1. HGK AIB AIHEE UZVGY OTZPI
   H ATG, HGK PITJ AIHEP SHEE
   IVA GHQB MBAJA: OTZ IB
   AIHEE AHWB IVA LBTLEB OZTQ
   PIBVZ AVGA.

2. SOQXK UTXIQYOXJ TI JNQL
   ROPF JNQXK, JNWJ NO BNQUN
   NWJN SOKMX W KTTY BTPA
   QX FTM BQGG VOPITPE QJ
   MXJQG JNO YWF TI COLML
   UNPQLJ.

3. KVP OAOPN UPOZHDPO VK EVQ
   CL EVVQ, ZYQ YVHBCYE HV WO
   POKDLOQ, CK CH WO
   POUOCAOQ FCHB HBZYILECACYE.

New Testament Headlines

1.

UNⒿUST, ⒿINFUL MAN COMMITS SⒿICIⒿE RATHER THAN ⒿSK FOR FORGIVENESS

— — — — —

2.

AMIDⒿT ⒿOYFⒿL THRONGS, HEAVⒿNLY KING RIDEⒿ DONKEY INTO EARTHLY CITY

— — — — —

3.

MAN SLICES OFF EAⒿ OF ARRⒿSTING SOLDIER WIⒿH SOLDIⒿR'S ⒿERSONAL SWORD

— — — — —

DANIEL 9:9

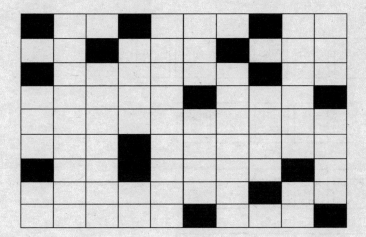

█			█				█		
		█				█			
█						█			
				█					█
		█							
█		█					█		
					█	█			
				█				█	

S	T	S	L	S	V	E	I	A	O
A	D	E	E	I	H	E	N	M	D
R	B	E	G	T	E	O	U	L	E
E	C	N	S	L	R	G	G	O	H
F	O	I	O	T	N	V	N	M	S
R	E	E	L	U	H	A	E	E	G
	W	R	L	H	A	D		G	R
	B	O		O	D	H		D	
	I			T					

Day
337

Mᴀʀᴛʏʀs

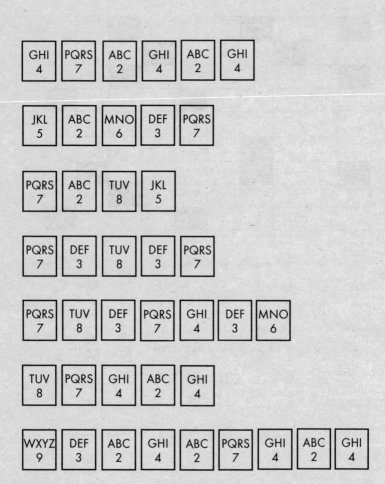

GHI 4	PQRS 7	ABC 2	GHI 4	ABC 2	GHI 4

JKL 5	ABC 2	MNO 6	DEF 3	PQRS 7

PQRS 7	ABC 2	TUV 8	JKL 5

PQRS 7	DEF 3	TUV 8	DEF 3	PQRS 7

PQRS 7	TUV 8	DEF 3	PQRS 7	GHI 4	DEF 3	MNO 6

TUV 8	PQRS 7	GHI 4	ABC 2	GHI 4

WXYZ 9	DEF 3	ABC 2	GHI 4	ABC 2	PQRS 7	GHI 4	ABC 2	GHI 4

Day
338

1. EOLHXC   VLO   THGXN   HT   VLO
   ZBU: THU   VLOA   NHG   YHV,
   YOBVLOU   CH   VLOA   UOZR,   YHU
   IZVLOU   BYVH   EZUYN;   AOV   AHFU
   LOZKOYXA   TZVLOU   TOOCOVL
   VLOS.   ZUO   AO   YHV   SFML
   EOVVOU   VLZY   VLOA?

2. ZGUIU   LW   MULZGUI   BUJ   MYI
   QIUUV,   ZGUIU   LW   MULZGUI
   FYMA   MYI   XIUU,   ZGUIU   LW
   MULZGUI   RPHU   MYI   XURPHU:
   XYI   EU   PIU   PHH   YMU   LM
   KGILWZ   BUWDW.

3. EIW   GIBWNQASQN   POIX
   RQWEQVHAG   HZLH   HZQ   KLG   IE
   HZQ   AIWK   NI   VITQHZ   LN   L
   HZJQE   JO   HZQ   OJUZH.

Scrambled Circles

1. NELAC
2. HISLPBU
3. DITHOLHW
4. RANEDW
5. SETORF
6. KDNRI
7. CALAEP
8. SONELISH

A dark and scary place for this prophet.

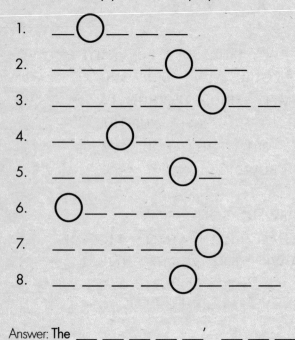

1. — ◯ — — —
2. — — — — ◯ — —
3. — — — — — ◯ — —
4. — — ◯ — — —
5. — — — — ◯ —
6. ◯ — — — —
7. — — — — — ◯
8. — — — — ◯ — — —

Answer: **The** __ __ __ __ __' __ __ __

Books of the Bible. . .

Sox due

— — — — — —

New Testament People. . .

Huey cuts

— — — — — — — —

Bad Guys. . .

This tin car

— — — — — — — — — —

CryptoScriptures

1. YRWQ NOQZQEPZQ NOS
   AQZWGDN GD IDMQZANGDMRDY
   OQGZN NP HIMYQ NOS JQPJXQ,
   NOGN R KGS MRABQZD
   UQNCQQD YPPM GDM UGM:
   EPZ COP RA GUXQ NP HIMYQ
   NORA NOS AP YZQGN G JQPJXQ?

2. AWERBJ ZBE XRPJQ GXBYE WFH
   ZJXC JX NXPBC QW YXRPC, BCH
   JX YXRPCXH RC AXYKEBFXT
   WCX BCH QJRYQG GXBYE.

3. RNE TRR EYN NTOEY WNTO EYN
   RMOF: RNE TRR EYN
   HUYTLHETUEX MW EYN QMORF
   XETUF HU TQN MW YHJ.

Day 342

MARK

Word	Clue	5-letter answer	Dropped
GERMANE	Combine	_____	1. __ __
ENDLESS	Snow vehicles	_____	2. __ __
DROWNED	Buzzing sound	_____	3. __ __
HEALING	Ascertain	_____	4. __ __
SWATTER	Scatter	_____	5. __ __
VARNISH	Pours down	_____	6. __ __
DIETARY	Unclean	_____	7. __ __
PLANTER	Future	_____	8. __ __
COOLEST	Clusters	_____	9. __ __
ANALECT	Scrub	_____	10. __ __
CHAMFER	Set up	_____	11. __ __
DEVOTEE	Chose	_____	12. __ __
ENDORSE	Compact	_____	13. __ __

___ ___ ___ ___ ___ ___ ___ ___ ___ ___ ___ ___ ___

___ ___ ___ ___ ___ ___ ___ ___ ___ ___ ___ ___ ___

1   2   3   4   5   6   7   8   9   10   11   12   13

Titus 3:9

	1	2	3	4	5
1	A	N	I	O	R
2	K	H	Y	S	C
3	E	F	B	M	Q
4	L	J	Z	D	V
5	T	U	G	W	P

33-52-51   11-45-14-13-44   32-14-14-41-13-24-22

35-52-31-24-51-13-14-12-24,   11-12-44

53-31-12-31-11-41-14-53-13-31-24,   11-12-44

25-14-12-51-31-12-51-13-14-12-24,   11-12-44

24-51-15-13-45-13-12-53-24   11-33-14-52-51

51-22-31   41-11-54;   32-14-15   51-22-31-23

11-15-31   52-12-55-15-14-32-13-51-11-33-41-31

11-12-44   45-11-13-12.

Romans 15:4

To go after

$\overline{17}$ $\overline{4}$ $\overline{31}$ $\overline{16}$ $\overline{10}$ $\overline{3}$

Predilection

$\overline{45}$ $\overline{5}$ $\overline{32}$ $\overline{14}$ $\overline{23}$ $\overline{1}$ $\overline{40}$ $\overline{34}$ $\overline{9}$ $\overline{42}$

Unnamed

$\overline{36}$ $\overline{15}$ $\overline{48}$ $\overline{24}$ $\overline{44}$ $\overline{39}$ $\overline{35}$ $\overline{41}$ $\overline{25}$

A chief angel

$\overline{47}$ $\overline{18}$ $\overline{43}$ $\overline{6}$ $\overline{26}$ $\overline{13}$ $\overline{22}$ $\overline{7}$ $\overline{30}$

An unbranded animal

$\overline{33}$ $\overline{8}$ $\overline{27}$ $\overline{19}$ $\overline{46}$ $\overline{12}$ $\overline{37}$ $\overline{50}$

Concerning the home or family

$\overline{28}$ $\overline{49}$ $\overline{11}$ $\overline{20}$ $\overline{38}$ $\overline{2}$ $\overline{29}$ $\overline{21}$

17-48-5   3-6-47-2-25-48-23-27-42-1   2-6-12-13-22-38

3-19-46-7   3-5-29-2-2-42-34   36-14-48-1-32-2-12-33-19

3-7-18-20   3-46-29-2-2-20-13   17-4-18   35-41-1

31-42-26-5-34-12-24-22,   2-6-8-2   3-19

2-6-5-4-41-22-6   45-36-2-29-32-15-43-19   8-13-28

21-49-39-14-4-1-2   10-17   2-6-32

25-37-18-12-45-2-41-5-23-38   11-29-22-6-2

6-36-27-42   6-10-45-32.

1. BAML
2. DLBESES
3. REROCTC
4. WOLFOL
5. INOZ

6. TEYBAU
7. NBRU
8. DJUEG
9. EBVEILE

Another name for Satan.

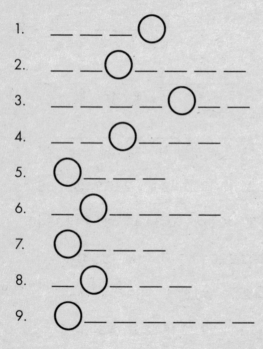

1. __ __ __ ◯
2. __ __ ◯ __ __ __ __
3. __ __ __ __ ◯ __ __
4. __ __ ◯ __ __ __
5. ◯ __ __ __
6. __ ◯ __ __ __ __
7. ◯ __ __ __
8. __ ◯ __ __ __
9. ◯ __ __ __ __ __ __

Answer: __ __ __ __ __ __ __ __ __

1. XVLF BS NIRN NIS ELCK IS UZ
QLK: UN UZ IS NIRN IRNI
WRKS JZ, RVK VLN FS
LJCZSEPSZ; FS RCS IUZ YSLYES,
RVK NIS ZISSY LA IUZ
YRZNJCS.

2. EHM KR YJC YVHDORO ZVS VHS
MSJDCFSRCCUVDC, KR YJC
ESHUCRO ZVS VHS UDUIHUMURC:
MKR TKJCMUCRXRDM VZ VHS
NRJTR YJC HNVD KUX; JDO
YUMK KUC CMSUNRC YR JSR
KRJGRO.

3. TU CGB HTWJ QX GTO CGLC
GLCG MUVBPJCLUVTUR DTJVQO
TJ XQMUV: FMC L PQV TJ XQP
CGB FLKZ QX GTO CGLC TJ
SQTV QX MUVBPJCLUVTUR.

New Testament Headlines

1.

**MA●S●VE EARTHQU●KE
FREES ●ESSER-KNOWN MAN
AND OTHERS FROM PRI●ON**

— — — — —

2.

**FIRS● MA● IN AC●AIA
FINALLY BELI●VES IN
GO●●EL'S S●VING ME●S●GE**

— — — — — — — — —

3.

**MAN PRO●EEDS TO
EP●ES●S AND VERBALL● GIVES
APOS●LE'S ●URRENT AFFA●R●**

— — — — — — — —

1 JOHN 5:4

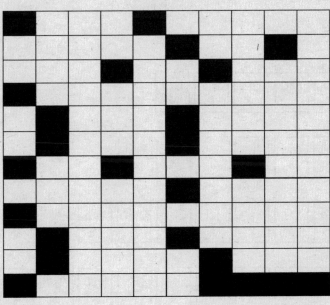

H	I	O	R	T	N	W	G	T	S
D	T	V	E	R	H	T	M	R	B
D	O	N	H	E	C	E	M	I	T
C	F	V	E	E	T	T	O	V	T
O	E	T	H	E	C	H	O	R	L
O	R	A	V	E	H	I	H	U	T
H	F	S	I	D	F	W	H	A	T
	O	O	T	W	W	O	A	E	L
		V	R	Y	O	O	S	O	S
		E	N	R	O		O	E	D
		T	O	O					R
		E		R					I
		A							

Gifts of the Holy Spirit

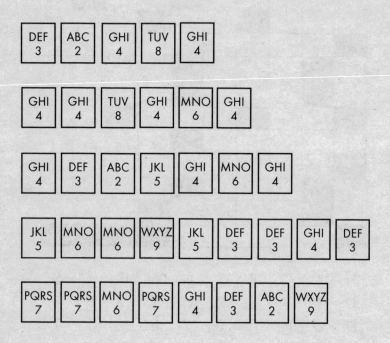

WOMEN OF THE BIBLE. . .

Ham art

_ _ _ _ _ _ _

PLACES. . .

Hog gloat

_ _ _ _ _ _ _ _ _

RIVERS/BODIES OF WATER. . .

Pure haste

_ _ _ _ _ _ _ _ _ _

1. EATTIMED   5. DHIAANMD

2. SAVEW   6. NIEM

3. HRTIG   7. TTTSESAU

4. ETLRBEM   8. SURCED

Chosen to replace Judas as one of the twelve spostles.

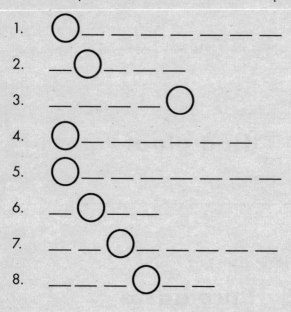

1. ◯__ __ __ __ __ __ __

2. __◯__ __ __

3. __ __ __ __◯

4. ◯__ __ __ __ __ __

5. ◯__ __ __ __ __ __

6. __◯__ __

7. __ __◯__ __ __ __

8. __ __ __◯__ __

Answer: __ __ __ __ __ __ __ __

Day
352

1. KIPR QMTW MRBXPZPL, XIMK
   HPMR FP KC XPPQ MRL KC
   DZPME HSRP IPMZK? ACZ S MH
   ZPMLF RCK KC DP DCTRL
   CRWF, DTK MWBC KC LSP MK
   NPZTBMWPH ACZ KIP RMHP CA
   KIP WCZL NPBTB.

2. WFY QT JZR ZWFY DTTHFY JZHH,
   KBJ QJ DTT: QJ QN PHJJHC TDC
   JZHH JD HFJHC QFJD AQTH
   VWQVHY, JZWF ZWUQFE JGD
   ZWFYN JD ED QFJD ZHAA, QFJD
   JZH TQCH JZWJ FHUHC NZWAA
   PH XBHFKZHY.

3. HJQL? SFWH TV FWL LJQL TWNE
   XWMT YU LJV LVIOBV WZ LJV
   JWBT DJWUL HJYGJ YU YF TWN,
   HJYGJ TV JQCV WZ DWM, QFM
   TV QEV FWL TWNE WHF?

New Testament Headlines

1.

●●D PRI●●ONER M●N CHOSEN TO GO F●EE ●Y PU●LIC DEM●ND

— — — — — — — —

2.

PILATE BEC●MES F●IEN●S WITH ●ATED EN●MY BECAUSE OF COMMON PRISONER

— — — — —

3.

MAN CAREFULLY ●NSTRUCTED IN HOW ●O PROPERLY ●TAR● A CH●RCH

— — — — —

1. SSSEITDR
2. MEADR
3. NESIO
4. RTEHDUN
5. YETPM
6. EBTEAD
7. KDNRI
8. LIDHC
9. RUNT

The governing council of the Jews.

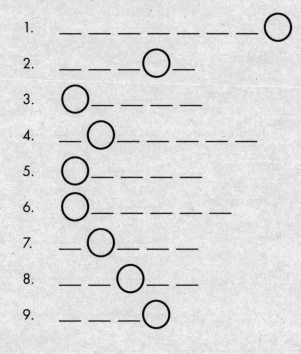

1. __ __ __ __ __ __ __ ⬤
2. __ __ __ ⬤ __
3. ⬤ __ __ __ __
4. __ ⬤ __ __ __ __ __
5. ⬤ __ __ __ __
6. ⬤ __ __ __ __
7. __ ⬤ __ __ __
8. __ __ ⬤ __ __
9. __ __ __ ⬤

Answer: __ __ __ __ __ __ __ __ __

1 JOHN

TRASHED	Cut off	_____	1. __ __
EUCHRED	Healed	_____	2. __ __
NEAREST	Trap	_____	3. __ __
TEACHER	Touch	_____	4. __ __
RAMBLER	Point finger	_____	5. __ __
UNEARTH	Valentine	_____	6. __ __
ASPIRED	Falls in drops	_____	7. __ __
GHASTLY	Hurriedly	_____	8. __ __
OCULATE	Sharp	_____	9. __ __
DEALING	Gather grain	_____	10. __ __
FEARING	Rule	_____	11. __ __
NASCENT	Bare	_____	12. __ __

— — — — — — — — — —

— — — — — — — — — — —

1 2 3 4 5 6 7 8 9 10 11 12

1 Timothy 6:12

	1	2	3	4	5
1	A	N	I	O	R
2	K	H	Y	S	C
3	E	F	B	M	Q
4	L	J	Z	D	V
5	T	U	G	W	P

32-13-53-22-51   51-22-31   53-14-14-44   32-13-53-22-51

14-32   32-11-13-51-22,   41-11-23   22-14-41-44   14-12

31-51-31-15-12-11-41   41-13-32-31....11-12-44

22-11-24-51   55-15-14-32-31-24-24-31-44   11

53-14-14-44   55-15-14-32-31-24-24-13-14-12

33-31-32-14-15-31   34-11-12-23

54-13-51-12-31-24-24-31-24.

Day
357

1 CORINTHIANS 2:9

A warning to be careful

$\overline{46}$ $\overline{25}$ $\overline{12}$ $\overline{39}$ $\overline{19}$ $\overline{3}$

Pardon

$\overline{24}$ $\overline{48}$ $\overline{6}$ $\overline{40}$ $\overline{51}$ $\overline{4}$ $\overline{33}$ $\overline{45}$ $\overline{18}$ $\overline{41}$ $\overline{11}$

A record of the past

$\overline{52}$ $\overline{26}$ $\overline{5}$ $\overline{20}$ $\overline{13}$ $\overline{47}$ $\overline{34}$

Something made better

$\overline{38}$ $\overline{21}$ $\overline{32}$ $\overline{2}$ $\overline{29}$ $\overline{43}$ $\overline{9}$ $\overline{15}$ $\overline{8}$ $\overline{36}$ $\overline{27}$

Apt to lie or cheat

$\overline{14}$ $\overline{42}$ $\overline{22}$ $\overline{1}$ $\overline{35}$ $\overline{50}$ $\overline{7}$ $\overline{28}$ $\overline{16}$

To keep up

$\overline{37}$ $\overline{23}$ $\overline{44}$ $\overline{10}$ $\overline{49}$ $\overline{30}$ $\overline{17}$ $\overline{31}$

46-28-20   39-5   26-27   44-41   12-2-26-20-27-1-10,

42-34-8   52-23-49-52   45-13-20   5-33-3-36,

31-29-47   42-23-19   52-33-23-2-14,

31-1-35-50-52-3-47   52-39-43-3   42-45-20-33-6-9-14

35-10-49-29   27-52-42   52-25-39-47-20   48-24

37-30-31,   27-52-18   20-52-51-45-40-11

12-52-38-22-52   40-29-14   52-39-49-52

32-47-3-32-23-2-18-14   7-29-2   20-52-9-21

50-52-30-49   16-13-4-1   52-17-15.

1. PPROREOSS   5. THREA
2. ROHEDSLU   6. SIMESND
3. NOREHT   7. TUCEISJ
4. DRIPE   8. ASRYI

It's not about reading the future, but about speaking the Word of God.

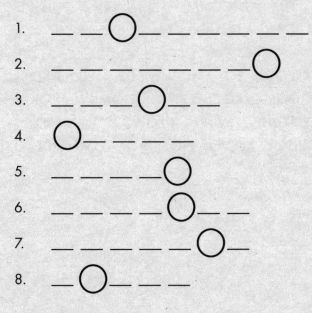

1. __ __ O __ __ __ __ __ __
2. __ __ __ __ __ __ __ O
3. __ __ __ O __ __
4. O __ __ __ __
5. __ __ __ __ O
6. __ __ __ __ O __ __
7. __ __ __ __ __ O __
8. __ O __ __ __

Answer: __ __ __ __ __ __ __ __

1. L DGBKTFTN YFHLU GN L PBFYU KF ZOB ZTNCLUJ: CTK NZO KZLK HLAOKZ LNZLHOJ GN LN BFKKOUUONN GU ZGN CFUON.

2. LJC HTQ, T UTMI, CKTJ PMC TJM ZPCKNM; QN PMN CKN SUPV, PHI CKTJ TJM DTCCNM; PHI QN PUU PMN CKN QTMO TZ CKV KPHI.

3. EQ KREQZ, EQ MUCUWOHP; EQYOFKQ TRFZ OGMQZKOZT PNQ GQMUW, OK O ZROZUHC WURH, XOWSQPN OERFP, KQQSUHC XNRA NQ AOT GQMRFZ.

New Testament Headlines

1.

**●ROMINENT MAN ●AS
DOC●OR FRIOND ST●DY
CORI●T●ANITY TH●ROUGH●Y**

— — — — — — — — —

2.

**R●LER DE●REE● A CENS●●
●O BE T●KEN TH●OU●HO●T
TH● V●●T L●ND**

— — — — —
— — — — — —

3.

**DIETY BECOMES
R●QUIRED ●ACRIFICE FOR
●INFULLY UN●UST H●MANS**

— — — — — —

JAMES 2:26

Letter bank:
```
O   B   R   S   O   S   S   I   T   H
I   U   O   I   T   L   F   S   S   P
A   R   T   D   A   I   W   A   D   D
H   A   R   K   Y   H   I   T   T   E
W   O   D   T   A   H   E   O   H   T
E   D   I   T   A   S   U   I   E
F   O   W       S       O
```

1. REDAC
2. DESOILP
3. DOLTHEA
4. NROKEB
5. KFCLO
6. YOGODL

7. ROECNR
8. IGNK
9. EVIGATN
10. TAPERD
11. TIMES

They believe our lives are controlled by something other than God.

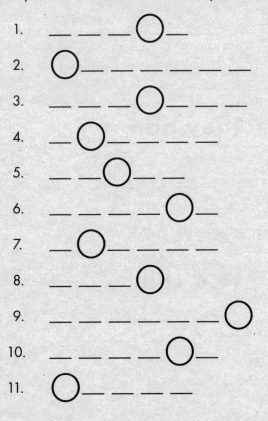

1. _ _ _ O _
2. O _ _ _ _ _ _
3. _ _ _ O _ _ _
4. _ O _ _ _ _
5. _ _ O _ _
6. _ _ _ _ O _
7. _ O _ _ _ _
8. _ _ _ O
9. _ _ _ _ _ _ O
10. _ _ _ _ O _
11. O _ _ _ _

Answer: _ _ _ _ _ _ _ _ _ _ _ _

BOOKS OF THE BIBLE. . .

Evict Luis

_ _ _ _ _ _ _ _ _

BIBLE CITIES. . .

They ban

_ _ _ _ _ _ _

PAUL'S MISSIONARY JOURNEYS. . .

to a chin

_ _ _ _ _ _ _

1. EKF   YCQKQ   QPDO,   QKVVCB
   UDFFUC   JXDUOBCH,   PHO
   VRBEDO   FXCG   HRF,   FR   JRGC
   KHFR   GC: VRB   RV   QKJX   DQ
   FXC   MDHLORG   RV   XCPSCH.

2. IDZ   RYVZV   MC   DWV   FDP,   QWP
   DWV   UVPMQRDZ   KVRNVVW   FDP
   QWP   UVW,   RYV   UQW   EYZMCR
   AVCLC.

3. EGK   MXDQ   RXSUGQYJKTXS   ZG
   HTKBXDK   RXUGKXDYSGYY;   JSW
   ZG   RXSKGSK   HTKB   YDRB
   KBTSVY   JY   MG   BJUG: OXQ   BG
   BJKB   YJTW,   T   HTEE   SGUGQ
   EGJUG   KBGG,   SXQ   OXQYJNG
   KBGG.

ANSWERS

Day 1: smile, cased, match, trace, range, Bible, beard, plume, cried, winds, singe, pound, Yukon: "Behold, I see the heavens opened" Acts 7:56.

Day 2: Wait on the LORD: be of good courage, and he shall strengthen thine heart: wait, I say, on the LORD.

Day 3: mark, flag, heavy, would, transcribe, persistence; Let us therefore follow after the things which make for peace, and things wherewith one may edify another.

Day 4: 1.Jesus 2.prophets 3.shadows 4.sandal 5.baptize 6.Naphtali 7.parable 8.spirit 9.Pharisees 10.beatitudes 11.salt; John the Baptist

Day 5: 1.For this is the message that ye heard from the beginning, that we should love one another (1 John 3:11). 2.In every thing give thanks: for this is the will of God in Christ Jesus concerning you (1 Thessalonians 5:18). 3.Thus saith the LORD the King of Israel, and his redeemer the LORD of hosts; I am the first, and I am the last; and beside me there is no God (Isaiah 44:6).

Day 6: 1.NASOSM, Samson 2.AHON, Noah 3.IDVDA, David

Day 7: In him was life; and the life was the light of men.

Day 8: Hagar, lioness, Sarah, vine, vineyard

Day 9: 1.diverse 2.time 3.flame 4.ancient 5.garment 6.plucked 7.exceeding 8.wheels; Immanuel

Day 10: lines, plush, elect, miter, frame, salve, parse, train, elate, cream, clear, fries, surge: "Surely he hath borne our griefs" Isaiah 53:4.

Day 11: Know ye not that ye are the temple of God, and that the Spirit of God dwelleth in you?

Day 12: thimble, working, itchy, overtime, transferred, useless; Therefore, my beloved brethren, be ye stedfast, unmoveable, always abounding in the work of the Lord.

Day 13: 1.persevere 2.pagans 3.brother 4.revelation 5.sins 6.fullness 7.fellowship; Ephesus

Day 14: 1.Thus saith the LORD, Let not the wise man glory in his wisdom, neither let the mighty man glory in his might, let not the rich man glory in his riches (Jeremiah 9:23). 2.And they that know thy name will put their trust in thee: for thou, LORD, hast not forsaken them that seek thee (Psalm 9:10). 3.For the preaching of the cross is to them that perish foolishness; but unto us which are saved it is the power of God (1 Corinthians 1:18).

Day 15: 1.BARMAHA, Abraham 2.SALU, Saul 3.AEDLIN, Daniel

Day 16: Sing unto the LORD; for he hath done excellent things: this is known in all the earth.

Day 17: Hoshea, Joseph, Paul, Peter, Samson, Silas, Simeon

Day 18: 1.master 2.beasts 3.seven 4.kingdom 5.roots 6.occasion 7.speak 8.reign; mandrake

Day 19: meals, savor, flora, bingo, piece, names, chief, parch, sheer, shoal, cleat, great, speed: "I will dwell in the midst of thee" Zechariah 2:10.

Day 20: But when I became a man, I put away childish things.

Day 21: cover, home, silent, plankton, wealthy, fondue; No man can serve two masters: for either he will hate the one, and love the other; or else he will hold to the one, and despise the other.

Day 22: 1.people 2.groaning 3.consider 4.sovereign 5.mercy 6.sinful 7.struggle 8.control 9.passions; Priscilla

Day 23: 1.Then Peter and the other apostles answered and said, We ought to obey God rather than men (Acts 5:29). 2.Take heed that ye do not your alms before men, to be seen of them: otherwise ye have no reward of your Father which is in heaven (Matthew 6:1). 3.And the LORD, he it is that doth go before thee; he will be with thee, he will not fail thee, neither forsake thee: fear not, neither be dismayed (Deuteronomy 31:8).

Day 24: 1.MDAA, Adam 2.SEOMS, Moses 3.JHAEIERM, Jeremiah

Day 25: I have no greater joy than to hear that my children walk in truth.

Day 26: Abraham, Esau, Isaac, Jesus, Joseph, Mary, Simeon

Day 27: 1.galleries 2.posts 3.leaven 4.between 5.stories 6.hundred 7.three 8.narrow 9.north 10.broad 11.cubit 12.head 13.chamber 14.arches; love one another

Day 28: taped, stair, stiff, goner, month, place, acted, dread, blade, glade, tents: "And he is before all things" Colossians 1:17.

Day 29: Let us hear the conclusion of the whole matter: Fear God, and keep his commandments: for this is the whole duty of man.

Day 30: clothes, whereabouts, niche, smorgasbord, spicy, story; Come now, and let us reason together, saith the LORD: though your sins be as scarlet, they shall be as white as snow.

Day 31: 1.baptize 2.wonder 3.sorcery 4.youth 5.declare 6.stricken 7.multiply 8.earth 9.hands; Zechariah

Day 32: 1.A man also or woman that hath a familiar spirit, or that is a wizard, shall surely be put to death: they shall stone them with stones: their blood shall be upon them (Leviticus 20:27). 2.And it shall come to pass, that from one new moon to another, and from one sabbath to another, shall all flesh come to worship before me, saith the LORD (Isaiah 66:23). 3.Take my yoke upon you, and learn of me; for I am meek and lowly in heart: and ye shall find rest unto your souls (Matthew 11:29).

Day 33: 1.ICNA, Cain 2.OHPJSE, Joseph 3.NOLOMOS, Solomon

Day 34: And, behold, I come quickly; and my reward is with me, to give every man according as his work shall be.

Day 35: bushel, cubit, denarius, drachma, omer, shekel, talent

Day 36: 1.groan 2.chestnut 3.lament 4.spread 5.hand 6.slain 7.garden 8.bound 9.shadow; guardians

Day 37: heats, plaid, toned, paper, taper, Tampa, after, spied, sheet, pairs, lying, ports: "The word of the Lord endureth" 1 Peter 1:25.

Day 38: For God hath not appointed us to wrath, but to obtain salvation by our Lord Jesus Christ.

Day 39: captivated, homework, foggy, crystal, optimistic, bunny; And he shall be like a tree planted by the rivers of water, that bringeth forth his fruit in his season.

Day 40: 1.people 2.great 3.increase 4.restore 5.devour 6.outcast 7.behold 8.pass 9.smite; Pentecost

Day 41: 1.But God commendeth his love toward us, in that, while we were yet sinners, Christ died for us (Romans 5:8). 2.All scripture is given by inspiration of God, and is profitable for doctrine, for reproof, for correction, for instruction in righteousness (2 Timothy 3:16). 3.I know that, whatsoever God doeth, it shall be for ever: nothing can be put to it, nor any thing taken from it: and God doeth it, that men should fear before him (Ecclesiastes 3:14).

Day 42: 1.HGAIGA, Haggai 2.RIZAEHHCA, Zechariah 3.ABMHAAR, Abraham

Day 43: To every thing there is a season, and a time to every purpose under the heaven.

Day 44: asp, camel, dove, eagle, fish, goat, lamb

Day 45: 1.sword 2.exalt 3.among 4.scatter 5.speak 6.stretch 7.ruin 8.rivers; Damascus

Day 46: basil, daily, store, peril, dense, spied, ennui, serum, space, stead, bland: "What doth the LORD require?" Micah 6:8

Day 47: Let no man despise thy youth; but be thou an example of the believers, in word, in conversation, in charity, in spirit, in faith, in purity.

Day 48: sleeves, maybe, family, wronged, thick, unified; There are, it may be, so many kinds of voices in the world, and none of them is without signification.

Day 49: 1.near 2.green 3.siege 4.rulers 5.girdles 6.sister 7.derision 8.contain 9.scatter 10.pity 11.house 12.heathen; resurrection

Day 50: 1. Teach me to do thy will; for thou art my God: thy spirit is good; lead me into the land of uprightness (Psalm 143:10). 2.And God shall wipe away all tears from their eyes; and there shall be no more death, neither sorrow, nor crying, neither shall there be any more pain: for the former things are passed away (Revelation 21:4). 3.So Christ was once offered to bear the sins of many; and unto them that look for him shall he appear the second time without sin unto salvation (Hebrews 9:28).

Day 51: 1.RSETHE, Esther 2.OMANI, Naomi 3.AJUSOH, Joshua

Day 52: Behold, the LORD's hand is not shortened, that it cannot save; neither his ear heavy, that it cannot hear.

Day 53: goat, grain, lamb, meal, meat, oil, son

Day 54: 1.profane 2.frontiers 3.glory 4.heathen 5.stately 6.bones 7.voice 8.dumb 9.prophesy; righteous

Day 55: learn, stole, winds, trees, amble, rated, glued, caned, noble, blasé, China, vines, verge: "The king made Daniel a great man" Daniel 2:48.

Day 56: And whatsoever ye do, do it heartily, as to the Lord, and not unto men.

Day 57: flame, young, Wisconsin, biography, caricature, diet; For ye are bought with a price: therefore glorify God in your body, and in your spirit, which are God's.

Day 58: 1.blessed 2.spirit 3.mourn 4.forbade 5.pinnacle; Simon

Day 59: 1.Not that which goeth into the mouth defileth a man; but that which cometh out of the mouth, this defileth a man (Matthew 15:11). 2.There is none holy as the LORD: for there is none beside thee: neither is there any rock like our God (1 Samuel 2:2). 3.In God I will praise his word, in God I have put my trust; I will not fear what flesh can do unto me (Psalm 56:4).

Day 60: 1.BAJCO, Jacob 2.SUEA, Esau 3.OLT, Lot

Day 61: Thou shalt have no other gods before me.

Day 62: Abraham, Cyrus, Darius, David, Jacob, Ruth, Samuel

Day 63: 1.flesh 2.manner 3.dealt 4.perish 5.execute 6.fallen 7.stretch 8.desire 9.despite 10.mourn 11.washed; Felix and Festus

Day 64: Bahia, Oprah, tills, grand, guest, lemon, their, riles, curds, piece, dealt, drawn, strap: "The LORD hath set a king over you." 1 Samuel 12:13

Day 65: Dearly beloved, avenge not yourselves, but rather give place unto wrath: for it is written, Vengeance is mine; I will repay, saith the Lord.

Day 66: flight, daytime, preview, pseudonym, scrutiny, rooster; If any man defile the temple of God, him shall God destroy; for the temple of God is holy, which temple ye are.

Day 67: 1.revile 2.Galilee 3.temple 4.country 5.angel 6.heard 7.rejoice 8.Herod 9.prison 10.pearl 11.blade; little child

Day 68: 1.Favour is deceitful, and beauty is vain: but a woman that feareth the LORD, she shall be praised (Proverbs 31:30). 2.And ye shall know that I am in the midst of Israel, and that I am the LORD your God, and none else: and my people shall never be ashamed (Joel 2:27). 3.And Jesus said unto them, I am the bread of life: he that cometh to me shall never hunger; and he that believeth on me shall never thirst (John 6:35).

Day 69: 1.EKEAHRB, Rebekah 2.EIADNI, Daniel 3.ZKHAEHEI, Hezekiah

Day 70: I will extol thee, my God, O king; and I will bless thy name for ever and ever.

Day 71: Bethshan, Damascus, Jericho, Jerusalem, Moab, Rabbah, Samaria

Day 72: 1.debtor 2.beget 3.branch 4.midst 5.eminent 6.toward 7.taken 8.broken 9.poor; tentmaker

Day 73: moose, scope, prate, shire, flute, court, inure, start, ceded, chair, piles, claim: "Who can judge this thy people?" 2 Chronicles 1:10

Day 74: The LORD is my light and my salvation; whom shall I fear? the LORD is the strength of my life; of whom shall I be afraid?

Day 75: duration, garbage, lawless, example, confirm, harmony; Do all things without murmurings and disputings.

Day 76: 1.Jesus 2.damsel 3.depart 4.time 5.receive 6.honor 7.kingdom; Jericho

Day 77: 1.The LORD is good, a strong hold in the day of trouble; and he knoweth them that trust in him (Nahum 1:7). 2.Let no corrupt communication proceed out of your mouth, but that which is good to the use of edifying, that it may minister grace unto the hearers (Ephesians 4:29). 3.But the Comforter, which is the Holy Ghost, whom the Father will send in my name, he shall teach you all things, and bring all things to your remembrance, whatsoever I have said unto you (John 14:26).

Day 78: 1.MLOOSON, Solomon 2.EMSOS, Moses 3.DGO, God

Day 79: Verily, verily, I say unto you, He that believeth on me hath everlasting life.

Day 80: deeds, frailties, needs, sorrows, thoughts, words

Day 81: 1.famine 2.under 3.taunt 4.ninety 5.country 6.high 7.statutes 8.siege; Eutychus

Day 82: weird, grits, Ravel, rival, shame, riled, miser, daily, eight, dense, dries, clank, sleds: "Why is the house of God forsaken?" Nehemiah 13:11

Day 83: For whether we live, we live unto the Lord; and whether we die, we die unto the Lord: whether we live therefore, or die, we are the Lord's.

Day 84: claustrophobia, defective, May, glutton, review, upstairs; Surely goodness and mercy shall follow me all the days of my life: and I will dwell in the house of the LORD for ever.

Day 85: 1.sheep 2.dancing 3.women 4.continued 5.capture 6.Philistine; Samuel

Day 86: 1.For as the heavens are higher than the earth, so are my ways higher than your ways, and my thoughts than your thoughts (Isaiah 55:9). 2.There shall not any man be able to stand before thee all the days of thy life: as I was with Moses, so I will be with thee: I will not fail thee, nor forsake thee (Joshua 1:5). 3.The LORD hath appeared of old unto me, saying, Yea, I have loved thee with an everlasting love: therefore with lovingkindness have I drawn thee (Jeremiah 31:3).

Day 87: 1.JLEAIH, Elijah 2.JSOHAI, Josiah 3.CJOAB, Jacob

Day 88: Yet I will rejoice in the LORD, I will joy in the God of my salvation.

Day 89: Aaron, Ananias, Annas, Eli, Ezra, Joshua, Zacharias

Day 90: 1.stone 2.enemy 3.young 4.arrow 5.against 6.shout 7.gravel 8.sought 9.quiver; synagogue

Day 91: trine, dirts, stray, loath, chain, mired, leash, bikes, malts, eager, legit: "Have joy of thee in the Lord" Philemon 1:20.

Day 92: Let all bitterness, and wrath, and anger, and clamour, and evil speaking, be put away from you, with all malice.

Day 93: muddy, clover, father, ghost, naughty, beneficiary; A good name is rather to be chosen than great riches, and loving favour rather than silver and gold.

Day 94: 1.Zidon 2.battle 3.rising 4.tribes 5.plains 6.strength 7.chariots 8.toward 9.death; Zarephath

Day 95: 1.Moreover whom he did predestinate, them he also called: and whom he called, them he also justified: and whom he justified, them he also glorified (Romans 8:30). 2.How excellent is thy lovingkindness, O God! therefore the children of men put their trust under the shadow of thy wings (Psalm 36:7). 3.And whosoever shall speak a word against the Son of man, it shall be forgiven him: but unto him that blasphemeth against the Holy Ghost it shall not be forgiven (Luke 12:10).

Day 96: 1.ARHSA, Sarah 2.AICSA, Isaac 3.NHSMAEAS, Manasseh

Day 97: A soft answer turneth away wrath: but grievous words stir up anger.

Day 98: Abdon, Deborah, Ehud, Gideon, Jair, Othniel, Tola

Day 99: 1.gnash 2.prophet 3.secret 4.covered 5.drunken 6.misery 7.destroy; sorcery

Day 100: files, tunic, prate, fable, earth, cowed, tiles, slain, evens, baste, black, paper, leaps: "Thou shalt love the LORD thy God" Deuteronomy 6:5.

Day 101: For every one that asketh receiveth; and he that seeketh findeth; and to him that knocketh it shall be opened.

Day 102: camouflage, winter, five, happy, adoration, listless; Even a fool, when he holdeth his peace, is counted wise: and he that shutteth his lips is esteemed a man of understanding.

Day 103: 1.above 2.Zaccur 3.judgment 4.workman 5.willing 6.service 7.bowls; Ezekiel

Day 104: 1.There is that maketh himself rich, yet hath nothing: there is that maketh himself poor, yet hath great riches (Proverbs 13:7). 2.Now we know that God heareth not sinners: but if any man be a worshipper of God, and doeth his will, him he heareth (John 9:31). 3.Blessed be God, even the Father of our Lord Jesus Christ, the Father of mercies, and the God of all comfort (2 Corinthians 1:3).

Day 105: 1.ZLEEEJB, Jezebel 2.AAANNM, Naaman 3.AREOJHM, Jehoram

Day 106: Take my yoke upon you, and learn of me; for I am meek and lowly in heart: and ye shall find rest unto your souls.

Day 107: Nicanor, Nicolas, Parmenas, Philip, Prochorus, Stephen, Timon

Day 108: 1.behold 2.watch 3.zealous 4.escape 5.brook 6.fury 7.ashes; Lazarus

Day 109: decal, frail, clear, prime, greed, hated, stead, corps, flute, homer, count, grain, grail: "My grace is sufficient for thee" 2 Corinthians 12:9.

Day 110: My brethren, count it all joy when ye fall into divers temptations.

Day 111: beautify, mend, waterlogged, undertaker, centennial, hesitant; But his delight is in the law of the LORD; and in his law doth he meditate day and night.

Day 112: 1.job 2.appointed 3.troops 4.terrors 5.pillars 6.Zebedee 7.exalted; baptize

Day 113: 1.O God, thou art my God; early will I seek thee: my soul thirsteth for thee, my flesh longeth for thee in a dry and thirsty land, where no water is (Psalm 63:1). 2.The woman shall not wear that which pertaineth unto a man, neither shall a man put on a woman's garment: for all that do so are abomination unto the LORD thy God (Deuteronomy 22:5). 3.And the LORD said unto Moses, I will do this thing also that thou hast spoken: for thou hast found grace in my sight, and I know thee by name (Exodus 33:17).

Day 114: 1.MEOSS, Moses 2.OJB, Job 3.MLESUETHHA, Methuselah

Day 115: That thou mayest walk in the way of good men, and keep the paths of the righteous.

Day 116: David, John, Joshua, Luke, Matthew, Samuel, Solomon

Day 117: 1.Gilead 2.violence 3.kindle 4.worship 5.enter 6.roofs 7.farther 8.fire 9.life 10.Lebanon 11.abide; lilies of the field

Day 118: lanai, tripe, green, teach, trips, share, train, snood, flair, aging, alarm, float, cribs: "A name which is above every name" Philippians 2:9.

Day 119: Put on the whole armour of God, that ye may be able to stand against the wiles of the devil.

Day 120: bewildered, hindrance, toothpaste, putty, flash, spirit; But thou, when thou prayest, enter into thy closet, and when thou hast shut thy door, pray to thy Father which is in secret.

Day 121: 1.consume 2.exalt 3.pleasure 4.servant 5.answer 6.worship 7.pasture; expanse

Day 122: 1.Before the mountains were brought forth, or ever thou hadst formed the earth and the world, even from everlasting to everlasting, thou art God (Psalm 90:2). 2.Though a sinner do evil an hundred times, and his days be prolonged, yet surely I know that it shall be well with them that fear God, which fear before him (Ecclesiastes 8:12). 3.And whatsoever ye do in word or deed, do all in the name of the Lord Jesus, giving thanks to God and the Father by him (Colossians 3:17).

Day 123: 1.ONJAH, Jonah 2.AHANHN, Hannah 3.HEIARZACH, Zechariah

Day 124: Mercy unto you, and peace, and love, be multiplied.

Day 125: Daniel, Esther, Genesis, Jeremiah, Numbers, Proverbs, Psalms

Day 126: 1.incense 2.amend 3.glean 4.revolt 5.burned 6.rapture 7.nation 8.wholly 9.friend; centurion

Day 127: lured, eaten, drags, posed, lends, eased, begin, flake, poise, rites, bring, drive, flare: "Therefore, brethren, stand fast" 2 Thessalonians 2:15.

Day 128: O ye sons of men, how long will ye turn my glory into shame? how long will ye love vanity, and seek after leasing?

Day 129: friend, imaginary, UT, buckle, swamp, glover; A word fitly spoken is like apples of gold in pictures of silver.

Day 130: 1.eaten 2.bones 3.terrible 4.hearth 5.righteous 6.ordinance 7.enemy; Abraham

Day 131: 1.The Lord knoweth how to deliver the godly out of temptations, and to reserve the unjust unto the day of judgment to be punished (2 Peter 2:9). 2.Keep yourselves in the love of God, looking for the mercy of our Lord Jesus Christ unto eternal life (Jude 1:21). 3.And Jesus looking upon them saith, With men it is impossible, but not with God: for with God all things are possible (Mark 10:27).

Day 132: 1.EDGION, Gideon 2.ZZNHUBECDARAEN, Nebuchadnezzar 3.DIDAV, David

Day 133: Thou art more glorious and excellent than the mountains of prey.

Day 134: anise, veal, fish, mint, mustard

Day 135: 1.blood 2.widow 3.swear 4.dust 5.falsely 6.stand 7.cause 8.playing 9.people 10.execute 11.round; The Lord's Supper

Day 136: fairs, train, roper, curse, means, realm, drain, doing, coral, agree, fared, "Go to the ant, thou sluggard" Proverbs 6:6.

Day 137: Wherefore, my dearly beloved, flee from idolatry.

Day 138: participate, adventure, flawless, mutter, authentic, onward; The words of the LORD are pure words: as silver tried in a furnace of earth, purified seven times.

Day 139: 1.Jeremiah 2.trouble 3.speak 4.neither 5.build 6.Tarshish; Joshua

Day 140: 1.It is good that a man should both hope and quietly wait for the salvation of the LORD (Lamentations 3:26). 2.For the day of the LORD is near upon all the heathen: as thou hast done, it shall be done unto thee: thy reward shall return upon thine own head (Obadiah 1:15). 3.And this is life eternal, that they might know thee the only true God, and Jesus Christ, whom thou hast sent (John 17:3).

Day 141: 1.TNOHBA, Naboth 2.AALMBA, Balaam 3.ZREA, Ezra

Day 142: For whosoever exalteth himself shall be abased; and he that humbleth himself shall be exalted.

Day 143: Ararat, Carmel, Hor, Horeb, Moriah, Olive, Sinai

Day 144: 1.thirst 2.showers 3.arise 4.plant 5.away 6.reject 7.prosper 8.change 9.kings; shipwreck

Day 145: close, plain, laced, lover, cling, steed, slant, least, rosin, regal, glide, shunt, stain: "To every thing there is a season" Ecclesiastes 3:1.

Day 146: Lift up your heads, O ye gates; even lift them up, ye everlasting doors; and the King of glory shall come in.

Day 147: politician, swirl, rhyme, doggie bag, turn, forget; Let the word of Christ dwell in you richly in all wisdom; teaching and admonishing one another in psalms and hymns and spiritual songs.

Day 148: 1.wilderness 2.country 3.wheat 4.weight 5.remember 6.lord 7.bracelet 8.Zion; Ruth and Boaz

Day 149: 1.I exhort therefore, that, first of all, supplications, prayers, intercessions, and giving of thanks, be made for all men (1 Timothy 2:1). 2.Beloved, follow not that which is evil, but that which is good. He that doeth good is of God: but he that doeth evil hath not seen God (3 John 1:11). 3.For the rod of the wicked shall not rest upon the lot of the righteous; lest the righteous put forth their hands unto iniquity (Psalm 125:3).

Day 150: 1.CEBLA, Caleb 2.LDIALEH, Delilah 3.INGDOE, Gideon

Day 151: Jesus Christ the same yesterday, and to day, and for ever.

Day 152: Aaron, David, Elijah, Elisha, Jacob, Moses, Solomon

Day 153: 1.portion 2.marry 3.forget 4.beauty 5.remember 6.sprinkle 7.grief; parable

Day 154: feint, stone, stile, shred, sting, final, creed, Latin, chase, grief, blurt, scone, scare: "Thou anointest my head with oil" Psalm 23:5.

Day 155: To the weak became I as weak, that I might gain the weak: I am made all things to all men, that I might by all means save some.

Day 156: Hyde, wrestle, buffalo, muggy, ancient, herbal; I will sing unto the LORD, because he hath dealt bountifully with me.

Day 157: 1.great 2.horses 3.jealous 4.midst 5.Jerusalem 6.plummet 7.hosts; Goliath

Day 158: 1.God is not a man, that he should lie; neither the son of man, that he should repent: hath he said, and shall he not do it? or hath he spoken, and shall he not make it good? (Numbers 23:19). 2.Let your heart therefore be perfect with the LORD our God, to walk in his statutes, and to keep his commandments, as at this day (1 Kings 8:61). 3.If thine enemy be hungry, give him bread to eat; and if he be thirsty, give him water to drink (Proverbs 25:21).

Day 159: 1.EJLA, Jael 2.EZZBSRHAAL, Belshazzar 3.HPARHOA, Pharaoh

Day 160: A double minded man is unstable in all his ways.

Day 161: angels, beauty, eternity, holiness, joy, perfection, unity

Day 162: 1.And God made the firmament, and divided the waters which were under the firmament from the waters which were above the firmament: and it was so (Genesis 1:7). 2.And the boys grew: and Esau was a cunning hunter, a man of the field; and Jacob was a plain man, dwelling in tents (Genesis 25:27). 3.As thou knowest not what is the way of the spirit, nor how the bones do grow in the womb of her that is with child: even so thou knowest not the works of God who maketh all (Ecclesiastes 11:5).

Day 163: chair, named, trams, blade, learn, agent, trick, waver, Paris, verso, barge, plane, reeds: "There is one body, and one Spirit" Ephesians 4:4.

Day 164: I will call upon the LORD, who is worthy to be praised: so shall I be saved from mine enemies.

Day 165: expensive, logical, bystander, whine, autograph, embrace; O LORD our Lord, how excellent is thy name in all the earth! who hast set thy glory above the heavens.

Day 166: 1.sinful 2.father 3.assemble 4.vision 5.gladness 6.brethren 7.faith 8.opened 9.found; salvation

Day 167: 1.Likewise, I say unto you, there is joy in the presence of the angels of God over one sinner that repenteth (Luke 15:10). 2.But God hath chosen the foolish things of the world to confound the wise; and God hath chosen the weak things of the world to confound the things which are mighty (1 Corinthians 1:27). 3.For the love of money is the root of all evil: which while some coveted after, they have erred from the faith, and pierced themselves through with many sorrows (1 Timothy 6:10).

Day 168: 1.HIAASI, Isaiah 2.LARSEI, Israel 3.MHNAA, Haman

Day 169: But he knoweth the way that I take: when he hath tried me, I shall come forth as gold.

Day 170: Cain, Canaan, ground, Jehoiachin, nature, serpent

Day 171: picky, swallowed, bump, gargle, chauffeur, nutritious; He that is slow to anger is better than the mighty; and he that ruleth his spirit than he that taketh a city.

Day 172: hotly, crate, canes, aural, doing, stark, spice, ratio, boles, stain, pride, capes: "But the tongue can no man tame" James 3:8.

Day 173: Boast not thyself of to morrow; for thou knowest not what a day may bring forth.

Day 174: Jesus saith unto him, I am the way, the truth, and the life: no man cometh unto the Father, but by me.

Day 175: 1.Samaria 2.remove 3:sepulchre 4.anointed 5.Bethlehem 6.covenant 7.captain; Solomon

Day 176: 1.Wherefore we receiving a kingdom which cannot be moved, let us have grace, whereby we may serve God acceptably with reverence and godly fear (Hebrews 12:28). 2.He is the Rock, his work is perfect: for all his ways are judgment: a God of truth and without iniquity, just and right is he (Deuteronomy 32:4). 3.He hath made the earth by his power, he hath established the world by his wisdom, and hath stretched out the heavens by his discretion (Jeremiah 10:12).

Day 177: 1.EEV, Eve 2.BJCAO, Jacob 3.UEALMS, Samuel

Day 178: Recompense to no man evil for evil. Provide things honest in the sight of all men.

Day 179: Abraham, Isaac, Israel, Jacob, Joshua, Moses, Noah

Day 180: Corinthians, Garden of Eden, Simon Peter

Day 181: quiet, doing, grave, reset, slice, chord, timed, scans, plate, raise, spins: "A new heaven and a new earth" Revelation 21:1.

Day 182: I will both lay me down in peace, and sleep: for thou, LORD, only makest me dwell in safety.

Day 183: high school, flavour, wiggle, calendar, recovery, market; The LORD is my rock, and my fortress, and my deliverer; my God, my strength, in whom I will trust.

Day 184: 1.compass 2.captive 3.desolate 4.Babylon 5.gravel 6.spanned 7.strait 8.ashamed; city gate

Day 185: 1.And be not conformed to this world: but be ye transformed by the renewing of your mind, that ye may prove what is that good, and acceptable, and perfect, will of God (Romans 12:2). 2.And a voice came out of the throne, saying, Praise our God, all ye his servants, and ye that fear him, both small and great (Revelation 19:5). 3.But without faith it is impossible to please him: for he that cometh to God must believe that he is, and that he is a rewarder of them that diligently seek him (Hebrews 11:6).

Day 186: 1.UEKL, Luke 2.NNAA, Anna 3.OJNH, John

Day 187: While it is said, To day if ye will hear his voice, harden not your hearts, as in the provocation.

Day 188: Anna, Elizabeth, Joseph, Mary, shepherds, Simeon, Zacharias

Day 189: Battle of Jericho, Genesis, Dead Sea

Day 190: lanky, cadet, spent, ravel, piled, raked, shear, raise, brave, Maine, local, broad, lines: "Blessed be the glory of the LORD" Ezekiel 3:12.

Day 191: But I keep under my body. . .lest that by any means, when I have preached to others, I myself should be a castaway.

Day 192: justice, balance, favors, damaged, wither, plural; Serve the LORD with fear, and rejoice with trembling

Day 193: 1.Jeremiah 2.double 3.born 4.hunters 5.driven 6.justice 7.carcasses 8.abhor; Adonijah

Day 194: 1.Behold, the LORD's hand is not shortened, that it cannot save; neither his ear heavy, that it cannot hear (Isaiah 59:1). 2.O God, thou art my God; early will I seek thee: my soul thirsteth for thee. . .in a dry and thirsty land, where no water is (Psalm 63:1). 3.Neither shalt thou lie with any beast to defile thyself therewith: neither shall any woman stand before a beast to lie down thereto: it is confusion (Leviticus 18:23).

Day 195: 1.LASU, Saul 2.TEREP, Peter 3.PSNTEEH, Stephen

Day 196: Who is he that overcometh the world, but he that believeth that Jesus is the Son of God?

Day 197: centurion, Herod, Joseph, Martha, Pharisees, Pilate

Day 198: Lamentations, Mary Magdalene, prodigal son

Day 199: heart, threw, fable, scale, caste, their, bread, Fords, verbs, least, trace, sight, champ: "Learn not the way of the heathen" Jeremiah 10:2.

Day 200: I will praise the LORD according to his righteousness: and will sing praise to the name of the LORD most high.

Day 201: guppy, lovable, kindergarten, astronomy, chef, nominate; Arise, O LORD; save me, O my God: for thou hast smitten all mine enemies upon the cheek bone.

Day 202: 1.famine 2.forgive 3.Judah 4.contend 5.vanity 6.forsaken 7.filled 8.inhabit 9.salvation 10.Jerusalem 11.priests; The Mount of Olives

Day 203: 1.Look not every man on his own things, but every man also on the things of others (Philippians 2:4). 2.And when Jesus had cried with a loud voice, he said, Father, into thy hands I commend my spirit: and having said thus, he gave up the ghost (Luke 23:46). 3.The eye that mocketh at his father, and despiseth to obey his mother, the ravens of the valley shall pick it out, and the young eagles shall eat it (Proverbs 30:17).

Day 204: 1.IEMAGALL, Gamaliel 2.OLEHC, Chloe 3.AULP, Paul

Day 205: And the world passeth away, and the lust thereof: but he that doeth the will of God abideth for ever.

Day 206: figs, garlic, grapes, honey, lamb, millet, olives

Day 207: Philemon, Pharisees, Herodias

Day 208: sheer, paned, bated, grant, going, forks, halos, brand, rated, using, stomp, cleat: "For I delight in the law of God" Romans 7:22.

Day 209: The thing that hath been, it is that which shall be; and that which is done is that which shall be done: and there is no new thing under the sun.

Day 210: farm, colander, honeymoon, labyrinth, PG movies, outgrow; Let the words of my mouth, and the meditation of my heart, be acceptable in thy sight, O LORD, my strength, and my redeemer.

Day 211: 1.Chaldeans 2.slain 3.rumor 4.violence 5.multitude 6.Jerusalem; Camels

Day 212: 1.Give unto the LORD the glory due unto his name: bring an offering, and come before him: worship the LORD in the beauty of holiness (1 Chronicles 16:29). 2.And God gave Solomon wisdom and understanding exceeding much, and largeness of heart, even as the sand that is on the sea shore (1 Kings 4:29). 3.I the LORD search the heart, I try the reins, even to give every man according to his ways, and according to the fruit of his doings (Jeremiah 17:10).

Day 213: 1.SJSEU, Jesus 2.IDAEORHS, Herodias 3.EONMSI, Simeon

Day 214: Because it is written, Be ye holy; for I am holy.

Day 215: Andrew, John, Judas, Peter, Philip, Simon, Thomas

Day 216: Thessalonians, Mount Ararat, Nineveh

Day 217: draft, grain, robin, lathe, there, ether, banal, scene, Tiber, brier, pains, cents, deter: "God, what shall we say after this?" Ezra 9:10

Day 218: Some trust in chariots, and some in horses: but we will remember the name of the LORD our God.

Day 219: Pacific, knuckle, extravagant, questionable, hardware, missionary; Be careful for nothing; but in every thing by prayer and supplication with thanksgiving let your requests be made known unto God.

Day 220: 1.smite 2.round 3.under 4.instruction 5.thick 6.sight 7.consume 8.Savior 9.remnant 10.rebuke; Mount Horeb

Day 221: 1.The thief cometh not, but for to steal, and to kill, and to destroy: I am come that they might have life, and that they might have it more abundantly (John 10:10). 2.For the husband is the head of the wife, even as Christ is the head of the church:

and he is the saviour of the body (Ephesians 5:23). 3.For all that is in the world, the lust of the flesh, and the lust of the eyes, and the pride of life, is not of the Father, but is of the world (1 John 2:16).

Day 222: 1.TPSBTHONTHJAIE, John the Baptist 2.LUAP, Paul 3.TSERMPEINO, Simon Peter

Day 223: For the LORD will not forsake his people for his great name's sake: because it hath pleased the LORD to make you his people.

Day 224: Ahiman, Anak, Goliath, Lahmi, Og, Sippai, Talmai

Day 225: Jeremiah, Rehoboam, Nicodemus

Day 226: stoop, cello, leans, darts, ruled, tied, aping, droll, mural, dined, cones, decal, gleam: "Unto God would I commit my cause" Job 5:8.

Day 227: I can do all things through Christ which strengtheneth me.

Day 228: weekday, embezzle, perfect, dugout, evaporate, fashion; Let nothing be done through strife or vainglory; but in lowliness of mind let each esteem other better than themselves.

Day 229: 1.Ezekiel 2.kingdom 3.Ethiopia 4.carbuncle 5.pharaoh 6.lifted 7.slain 8.terrible 9.judge 10.reproach 11.heathen; Enoch, Elijah

Day 230: 1.Be still, and know that I am God: I will be exalted among the heathen, I will be exalted in the earth (Psalm 46:10). 2.He that is slow to anger is better than the mighty; and he that ruleth his spirit than he that taketh a city (Proverbs 16:32). 3.Jesus answered, Verily, verily, I say unto thee, Except a man be born of water and of the Spirit, he cannot enter into the kingdom of God (John 3:5).

Day 231: 1.YMTOTIH, Timothy 2.USEOMSIN, Onesimus 3.TERPE, Peter

Day 232: Being confident of this very thing, that he which hath begun a good work in you will perform it until the day of Jesus Christ.

Day 233: castanets, drum, harp, lyre, organ, trumpet, zither

Day 234: Creation, Timothy, Bartimaeus

Day 235: cares, tying, learn, sales, final, Milan, throe, maids, carts, grain, singe, bleat: "Thy people shall by my people" Ruth 1:16.

Day 236: Love your enemies, bless them that curse you, do good to them that hate you, and pray for them which despitefully use you, and persecute you.

Day 237: vat, choreography, despair, working, misbelief, origami; The heavens declare the glory of God; and the firmament sheweth his handywork.

Day 238: 1.burning 2.season 3.matter 4.thousand 5.Persians 6.signet 7.early; Bethany

Day 239: 1.Blessed is the man that endureth temptation: for when he is tried, he shall receive the crown of life, which the Lord hath promised to them that love him (James 1:12). 2.But unto you that fear my name shall the Sun of righteousness arise with healing in his wings; and ye shall go forth, and grow up as calves of the stall (Malachi 4:2). 3.For God sent not his Son into the world to condemn the world; but that the world through him might be saved (John 3:17).

Day 240: 1.ANBBRAAS, Barnabas 2.RHDOE, Herod 3.AMOTSH, Thomas

Day 241: It is God that girdeth me with strength, and maketh my way perfect.

Day 242: Bethlehem, Corinth, Jerusalem, Nazareth, Rome, Tarsus

Day 243: Galatians, Good Samaritan, Mediterranean

Day 244: lease, clerk, quint, seeds, giant, sided, snore, agent, warms, thorn, court, drawn: "Bear ye one another's burdens" Galatians 6:2.

Day 245: Every word of God is pure: he is a shield unto them that put their trust in him.

Day 246: window, hindsight, viable, March, guiltless, headache; Let love be without dissimulation. Abhor that which is evil; cleave to that which is good.

Day 247: 1.plowed 2.Bethel 3.divided 4.incense 5.images 6.return 7.branches 8.depart 9. derision; Leviathan

Day 248: 1.Thou shalt not take the name of the LORD thy God in vain; for the LORD will not hold him guiltless that taketh his name in vain (Exodus 20:7). 2.And there arose not a prophet since in Israel like unto Moses, whom the LORD knew face to face (Deuteronomy 34:10). 3.And the Lord shall deliver me from every evil work, and will preserve me unto his heavenly kingdom: to whom be glory for ever and ever. Amen (2 Timothy 4:18).

Day 249: 1.RUASALZ, Lazarus 2.COIEUSMDN, Nicodemus 3.AGUSI, Gaius

Day 250: And ye shall seek me, and find me, when ye shall search for me with all your heart.

Day 251: Canaanite, centurion, leper, Martha, Paul, publican, Samaritan

Day 252: Judas Iscariot, Zechariah, Mount of Olives

Day 253: croon, bated, drain, caper, crime, being, vials, lines, dream, carts, skied, amber, stile: "Thou hast sent me into the world" John 17:18.

Day 254: If any of you lack wisdom, let him ask of God, that giveth to all men liberally, and upbraideth not; and it shall be given him.

Day 255: revenge, chair, amputate, wooden, free, blame; Be not overcome of evil, but overcome evil with good.

Day 256: 1.judgment 2.hemlock 3.graven 4.pursue 5.mischief 6.fallow 7.tumult 8.reaped 9.murder; Jerusalem

Day 257: 1.So then because thou art lukewarm, and neither cold nor hot, I will spue thee out of my mouth (Revelation 3:16). 2.And now why tarriest thou? arise, and be baptized, and wash away thy sins, calling on the name of the Lord (Acts 22:16). 3.Ye shall diligently keep the commandments of the LORD your God, and his testimonies, and his statutes, which he hath commanded thee (Deuteronomy 6:17).

Day 258: 1.REPTE, Peter 2.EUSJS, Jesus 3.RTDEESPOHI, Diotrephes

Day 259: But it is good for me to draw near to God: I have put my trust in the Lord GOD, that I may declare all thy works.

Day 260: Almighty, Blessed, Messiah, Prince, Redeemer, Saviour, Shepherd

Day 261: Damascus, Deuteronomy, Mesopotamia

Day 262: teach, later, there, heard, laced, mayor, their, flare, topic, dream, mends, waste, toils: "Holding fast the faithful word" Titus 1:9.

Day 263: Lead me, O LORD, in thy righteousness because of mine enemies; make thy way straight before my face.

Day 264: tickle, dragon, folly, wishbone, agriculture, protective; Whether therefore ye eat, or drink, or whatsoever ye do, do all to the glory of God.

Day 265: 1.Obadiah 2.stubble 3.mighty 4.remain 5.fields 6.thirst 7.prevail 8.breaches; Athaliah

Day 266: 1.Only fear the LORD, and serve him in truth with all your heart: for consider how great things he hath done for you (1 Samuel 12:24). 2.Nevertheless for thy great mercies' sake thou didst not utterly consume them, nor forsake them; for thou art a gracious and merciful God (Nehemiah 9:31). 3.And we know that all things work together for good to them that love God, to them who are the called according to his purpose (Romans 8:28).

Day 267: 1.YMRA, Mary 2.GRMEMNAYEALAD, Mary Magdalene 3.CEENUI, Eunice

Day 268: Set your affection on things above, not on things on the earth.

Day 269: Babylon, Bethel, Damascus, Gaza, Jericho, Nineveh, Samaria

Day 270: Malachi, Elisabeth, Agrippa

Day 271: grand, vines, under, medal, frame, Latin, dread, write, slims, gamin, boned, hedge, stare: "God created man in his own image" Genesis 1:27.

Day 272: Know ye not that they which run in a race run all, but one receiveth the prize? So run, that ye may obtain.

Day 273: tuxedo, jewelry, zoology, fabric, path, submarine; For by one Spirit are we all baptized into one body, whether we be Jews or Gentiles, whether we be bond or free.

Day 274: 1.dedicate 2.written 3.governor 4.servant 5.river 6.building 7.upon 8.sedition; denarius

Day 275: 1.Be careful for nothing; but in every thing by prayer and supplication with thanksgiving let your requests be made known unto God (Philippians 4:6). 2.Herein is love, not that we loved God, but that he loved us, and sent his Son to be the propitiation for our sins (1 John 4:10). 3.And he said to them all, If any man will come after me, let him deny himself, and take up his cross daily, and follow me (Luke 9:23).

Day 276: 1.UDASJ, Judas 2.AAPRGPI, Agrippa 3.NANAIAS, Ananias

Day 277: For they that are after the flesh do mind the things of the flesh; but they that are after the Spirit the things of the Spirit.

Day 278: Abraham, Adam, David, Isaac, Jonah, Moses, Noah

Day 279: Colossians, Delilah, Last Supper

Day 280: trade, plant, tease, alarm, refer, heart, later, satin, tough, creak, frees, amiss, slain: "For the LORD thy God is with thee" Joshua 1:9.

Day 281: To every thing there is a season, and a time to every purpose under the heaven.

Day 282: hurricane, fitness, magic, periwinkle, vulnerable, yonder; Even as I please all men in all things, not seeking mine own profit, but the profit of many, that they may be saved.

Day 283: 1.Levites 2.Passover 3.lambs 4.timber 5.rams 6.number 7.Darius 8.decree 9.killed 10.seven; tabernacle

Day 284: 1.And the LORD God said unto the woman, What is this that thou hast done? And the woman said, The serpent beguiled me, and I did eat (Genesis 3:13). 2.The fathers shall not be put to death for the children, neither shall the children be put to death for the fathers: every man shall be put to death for his own sin (Deuteronomy 24:16). 3.I will praise thee; for I am fearfully and wonderfully made: marvellous are thy works; and that my soul knoweth right well (Psalm 139:14).

Day 285: 1.ARNEDW, Andrew 2.MALESO, Salome 3.AIARSHPP, Sapphira

Day 286: I will say of the LORD, He is my refuge and my fortress: my God; in him will I trust.

Day 287: eternal, gracious, holy, infinite, just, merciful, wise

Day 288: Jericho, Pontius Pilate, Onesimus

Day 289: drone, stomp, grain, eater, dined, place, tardy, prose, grate, moist, throe: "I am with you, saith the LORD" Haggai 1:13.

Day 290: Be kindly affectioned one to another with brotherly love; in honour preferring one another.

Day 291: temperament, extra, howled, umbrella, strategic, yourself; All things are lawful unto me, but all things are not expedient: all things are lawful for me, but I will not be brought under the power of any.

Day 292: 1.cubit 2.publish 3.pine 4.brought 5.divide 6.waters 7.portions 8.Egypt 9.grieved; cupbearer

Day 293: 1.And immediately the angel of the Lord smote him, because he gave not God the glory: and he was eaten of worms, and gave up the ghost (Acts 12:23). 2.For the weapons of our warfare are not carnal, but mighty through God to the pulling down of strong holds (2 Corinthians 10:4). 3.He that covereth his sins shall not prosper: but whoso confesseth and forsaketh them shall have mercy (Proverbs 28:13).

Day 294: 1.PTEALI, Pilate 2.EATTWHM, Matthew 3.HACCAZUSE, Zacchaeus

Day 295: For the Lord giveth wisdom: out of his mouth cometh knowledge and understanding.

Day 296: Barnabas, James, Jude, Peter, Philip, Silas, Timothy

Day 297: Ephesians, Passover, Numbers

Day 298: leach, chair, grade, trash, feast, eaten, carve, great, yeast, place, dunes, singe, cubed: "Many shall rejoice at his birth" Luke 1:14.

Day 299: Remember not the sins of my youth, nor my transgressions: according to thy mercy remember thou me for thy goodness' sake, O LORD.

Day 300: suitable, courteous, increasingly, deep, waffle, khaki; We are fools for Christ's sake, but ye are wise in Christ; we are weak, but ye are strong; ye are honourable, but we are despised.

Day 301: 1.troops 2.heaven 3.vanish 4.deliver 5.evident 6.commit 7.possess 8.discern; Philemon

Day 302: 1.And he took bread, and gave thanks, and brake it, and gave unto them, saying, This is my body which is given for you: this do in remembrance of me (Luke 22:19). 2.In my Father's house are many mansions: if it were not so, I would have told you. I go to prepare a place for you (John 14:2). 3.For the eyes of the LORD run to and fro throughout the whole earth, to shew himself strong in the behalf of them whose heart is perfect toward him (2 Chronicles 16:9).

Day 303: 1.ITASAPN, Antipas 2.MOISN, Simon 3.UMATBIARSE, Bartimaeus

Day 304: Nay, in all these things we are more than conquerors through him that loved us.

Day 305: Acts, Hebrews, Jude, Matthew, Revelation, Romans, Titus

Day 306: Ecclesiastes, Jerusalem, Sanhedrin

Day 307: foreigner, October, matinee, vengeful, hidden, impossible; For to this end Christ both died, and rose, and revived, that he might be Lord both of the dead and living.

Day 308: 1.content 2.arrows 3.tossing 4.loathsome 5.clothed 6.comfort 7.return 8.rewards; cast lots

Day 309: 1.And the woman bare a son, and called his name Samson: and the child grew, and the LORD blessed him (Judges 13:24). 2.It is of the LORD's mercies that we are not consumed, because his compassions fail not. They are new every morning: great is thy faithfulness (Lamentations 3:22–23). 3.Let your speech be alway with grace, seasoned with salt, that ye may know how ye ought to answer every man (Colossians 4:6).

Day 310: steed, caked, sales, tread, tense, fling, soles, spoil, elite, pined, shape, borer, dames: "Now the just shall live by faith" Hebrews 10:38.

Day 311: Be kindly affectioned one to another with brotherly love; in honour preferring one another.

Day 312: valid, Christian, golf, hospitality, workout, barometer; For it is written, As I live, saith the Lord, every knee shall bow to me, and every tongue shall confess to God.

Day 313: 1.perverse 2.hireling 3.tongue 4.imagine 5.tokens 6.wrath 7.declare 8.increase 9.blown 10.anger; signet ring

Day 314: 1.Therefore being justified by faith, we have peace with God through our Lord Jesus Christ (Romans 5:1). 2.Jesus said unto her, I am the resurrection, and the life: he that believeth in me, though he were dead, yet shall he live (John 11:25). 3.Confess your faults one to another, and pray one for another, that ye may be healed. The effectual fervent prayer of a righteous man availeth much (James 5:16).

Day 315: 1.JSOHPE, Joseph 2.AMRATH, Martha 3.IALQUA, Aquila

Day 316: Whether therefore ye eat, or drink, or whatsoever ye do, do all to the glory of God.

Day 317: fish, goat, horse, locust, serpent, sheep, sparrow

Day 318: 1.troops 2.harvest 3.wicked 4.lies 5.wine 6.robbers 7.consent 8.midst 9.know 10.former 11.sour; Philistines

Day 319: Revelation, Rebekah, Macedonia

Day 320: react, trash, louse, noble, topic, slant, aping, timed, cited, Morse, prays, print: "For he is like a refiner's fire" Malachi 3:2.

Day 321: I will be glad and rejoice in thee: I will sing praise to thy name, O thou most High.

Day 322: impersonal, olfactory, barbecue, dawn, kings, hypothetical; Know ye not that your bodies are the members of Christ? shall I then take the members of Christ, and make them the members of an harlot? God forbid.

Day 323: 1.purity 2.hasten 3.captivity 4.needy 5.trust 6.mouth 7.perish; papyrus

Day 324: 1.But as for you, ye thought evil against me; but God meant it unto good, to bring to pass, as it is this day, to save much people alive (Genesis 50:20). 2.And of every living thing of all flesh, two of every sort shalt thou bring into the ark, to keep them alive with thee; they shall be male and female (Genesis 6:19). 3.And the Lord went before them by day in a pillar of a cloud, to lead them the way; and by night in a pillar of fire, to give them light; to go by day and night (Exodus 13:21).

Day 325: 1.DIAYL, Lydia 2.PLPIHI, Philip 3.UIERSTT, Tertius

Day 326: Now faith is the substance of things hoped for, the evidence of things not seen.

Day 327: David, Elisha, Ezra, Gideon, Moses, Noah, Samuel

Day 328: 1.servant 2.return 3.backward 4.shepherd 5.vanity 6.shout 7.built 8.foolish 9.down 10.spring; traditions

Day 329: 1.Behold, thou art fair, my love; behold, thou art fair; thou hast doves' eyes within thy locks: thy hair is as a flock of goats, that appear from mount Gilead (Song of Solomon 4:1). 2.And the vessel that he made of clay was marred in the hand of the potter: so he made it again another vessel, as seemed good to the potter to make it (Jeremiah 18:4). 3.Daniel answered and said, Blessed be the name of God for ever and ever: for wisdom and might are his (Daniel 2:20).

Day 330: Sodom, Nebuchadnezzar, Transfiguration

Day 331: tread, grips, treed, sweet, brain, rains, stork, hired, lunge, drain, table, sines: "Charity vaunteth not itself" 1 Corinthians 13:4.

Day 332: Let no man deceive himself. If any man among you seemeth to be wise in this world, let him become a fool, that he may be wise.

Day 333: hyperbole, favorite, scarlet, communication, walk, purchased; Therefore let us keep the feast, not with old leaven, neither with the leaven of malice and wickedness; but with the unleavened bread of sincerity and truth.

Day 334: 1.burden 2.smoother 3.drawn 4.attend 5.sacrifice 6.destroy 7.butter 8.wander 9.deceit 10.enemies; beatitudes

Day 335: 1.And she shall bring forth a son, and thou shalt call his name JESUS: for he shall save his people from their sins (Matthew 1:21). 2.Being confident of this very thing, that he which hath begun a good work in you will perform it until the day of Jesus Christ (Philippians 1:6). 3.For every creature of God is good, and nothing to be refused, if it be received with thanksgiving (1 Timothy 4:4).

Day 336: 1.JSUDA, Judas 2.SJUES, Jesus 3.RETEP, Peter

Day 337: To the Lord our God belong mercies and forgivenesses, though we have rebelled against him.

Day 338: Isaiah, James, Paul, Peter, Stephen, Uriah, Zechariah

Day 339: 1.Behold the fowls of the air: for they sow not, neither do they reap, nor gather into barns; yet your heavenly Father feedeth them. Are ye not much better than they (Matthew 6:26)? 2.There is neither Jew nor Greek, there is neither bond nor free, there is neither male nor female: for ye are all one in Christ Jesus (Galatians 3:28). 3.For yourselves know perfectly that the day of the Lord so cometh as a thief in the night (1 Thessalonians 5:2).

Day 340: 1.clean 2.publish 3.withhold 4.wander 5.forest 6.drink 7.palace 8.holiness; The lions' den

Day 341: Exodus, Eutychus, Antichrist

Day 342: 1.Give therefore thy servant an understanding heart to judge thy people, that I may discern between good and bad: for who is able to judge this thy so great a people (1 Kings 3:9)? 2.Josiah was eight years old when he began to reign, and he reigned in Jerusalem one and thirty years (2 Chronicles 34:1). 3.Let all the earth fear the Lord: let all the inhabitants of the world stand in awe of him (Psalm 33:8).

Day 343: merge, sleds, drone, glean, strew, rains, dirty, later, clots, clean, frame, voted, dense: "And have peace one with another" Mark 9:50.

Day 344: But avoid foolish questions, and genealogies, and contentions, and strivings about the law; for they are unprofitable and vain.

Day 345: follow, preference, anonymous, archangel, maverick, domestic; For whatsoever things were written aforetime were written for our learning, that we through patience and comfort of the scriptures might have hope.

Day 346: 1.lamb 2.blessed 3.correct 4.follow 5.Zion 6.beauty 7.burn 8.judge 9.believe; Beelzebub

Day 347: 1.Know ye that the LORD he is God: it is he that hath made us, and not we ourselves; we are his people, and the sheep of his pasture (Psalm 100:3). 2.But he was wounded for our transgressions, he was bruised for our iniquities: the chastisement of our peace was upon him; and with his stripes we are healed (Isaiah 53:5). 3.In the lips of him that hath understanding wisdom is found: but a rod is for the back of him that is void of understanding (Proverbs 10:13).

Day 348: 1.SIALS, Silas 2.TNHESPASA, Stephanas 3.CHUYTCIS, Tychicus

Day 349: For whatsoever is born of God overcometh the world: and this is the victory that overcometh the world, even our faith.

Day 350: faith, giving, healing, knowledge, prophecy

Day 351: Martha, Golgotha, Euphrates

Day 352: 1.meditate 2.waves 3.right 4.tremble 5.handmaid 6.mine 7.statutes 8.cursed; Matthias

Day 353: 1.Then Paul answered, What mean ye to weep and to break mine heart? for I am ready not to be bound only, but also to die at Jerusalem for the name of the Lord Jesus (Acts 21:13). 2.And if thy hand offend thee, cut if off: it is better for thee to enter into life maimed, than having two hands to go into hell, into the fire that never shall be quenched (Mark 9:43). 3.What? know ye not that your body is the temple of the Holy Ghost which is in you, which ye have of God, and ye are not your own (1 Corinthians 6:19)?

Day 354: 1.BASARBBA, Barabbas 2.ORDHE, Herod 3.ITSTU, Titus

Day 355: 1.distress 2.dream 3.noise 4.thunder 5.empty 6.debate 7.drink 8.child 9.turn; Sanhedrin

Day 356: shear, cured, snare, reach, blame, heart, drips, hasty, acute, glean, reign, scant: "The true God, and eternal life" 1 John 5:20.

Day 357: Fight the good fight of faith, lay hold on eternal life. . .and hast professed a good profession before many witnesses. 1 Timothy 6:12

Day 358: beware, forgiveness, history, improvement, deceitful, maintain; But as it is written, Eye hath not seen, nor ear heard, neither have entered into the heart of man, the things which God hath prepared for them that love him.

Day 359: 1.oppressor 2.shoulder 3.throne 4.pride 5.earth 6.dimness 7.justice 8.Syria; prophecy

Day 360: 1.A virtuous woman is a crown to her husband: but she that maketh ashamed is as rottenness in his bones (Proverbs 12:4). 2.But now, O LORD, thou art our father; we are the clay, and thou our potter; and we all are the work of thy hand (Isaiah 64:8). 3.Be sober, be vigilant; because your adversary the devil, as a roaring lion, walketh about, seeking whom he may devour (1 Peter 5:8).

Day 361: 1.PHTEUHSIOL, Theophilus 2.UCSUSTARGUEASA, Caesar Augustus 3.ESSJU, Jesus

Day 362: For as the body without the spirit is dead, so faith without works is dead also.

Day 363: 1.cedar 2.spoiled 3.loathed 4.broken 5.flock 6.goodly 7.corner 8.king 9.vintage 10.depart 11.smite; astrologers

Day 364: Leviticus, Bethany, Antioch

Day 365: 1.But Jesus said, Suffer little children, and forbid them not, to come unto me: for of such is the kingdom of heaven (Matthew 19:14). 2.For there is one God, and one mediator between God and men, the man Christ Jesus (1 Timothy 2:5). 3.Let your conversation be without covetousness; and be content with such things as ye have: for he hath said, I will never leave thee, nor forsake thee (Hebrews 13:5).